get real,
GET RICH

get real, GET RICH

CONQUER THE 7 LIES BLOCKING YOU FROM SUCCESS

FARRAH GRAY

DUTTON

DUTTON
Published by Penguin Group (USA) Inc.
375 Hudson Street, New York, New York 10014, U.S.A.

Penguin Group (Canada), 90 Eglinton Avenue East, Suite 700, Toronto, Ontario M4P
2Y3, Canada (a division of Pearson Penguin Canada Inc.); Penguin Books Ltd, 80 Strand,
London WC2R 0RL, England; Penguin Ireland, 25 St Stephen's Green, Dublin 2, Ire-
land (a division of Penguin Books Ltd); Penguin Group (Australia), 250 Camberwell
Road, Camberwell, Victoria 3124, Australia (a division of Pearson Australia Group Pty
Ltd); Penguin Books India Pvt Ltd, 11 Community Centre, Panchsheel Park, New
Delhi—110 017, India; Penguin Group (NZ), 67 Apollo Drive, Rosedale, North Shore
0632, New Zealand (a division of Pearson New Zealand Ltd); Penguin Books (South
Africa) (Pty) Ltd, 24 Sturdee Avenue, Rosebank, Johannesburg 2196, South Africa

Penguin Books Ltd, Registered Offices: 80 Strand, London WC2R 0RL, England

Published by Dutton, a member of Penguin Group (USA) Inc.

First printing, January 2008
1   3   5   7   9   10   8   6   4   2

REGISTERED TRADEMARK—MARCA REGISTRADA

LIBRARY OF CONGRESS CATALOGING-IN-PUBLICATION DATA HAS BEEN APPLIED FOR.

ISBN 978-0-525-95044-8

Printed in the United States of America
Set in Janson Text

In loving memory
and with supreme gratitude
to my sister, Greek Gray:
Her luminous and exquisite example
inspires us all to realize our
infinite potential in every moment

Truth can be stranger than fiction.

CONTENTS

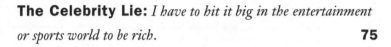

INTRODUCTION

Get Real, Get Rich

*Everybody wants to go to heaven but nobody wants to die.
Everybody wants success but not everyone is willing to do
what it takes to get there.*

Whenever I repeat those two sentences in front of an audience, the response is very similar. I sense a collective silence as people think about what those statements mean, quickly realizing how true they really are. You may have recognized the first statement; it's heard in many song lyrics, and no one knows who originally authored it. The second one is my own, and I don't intend to intimidate you by it. But it's true; no one becomes successful out of luck or through an easy 1-2-3 set of steps. Let's get one thing straight: If it were that easy, then virtually everyone would be rich and you probably would not be reading this. (Or maybe you are successful already, and your friends would say you've "made it." Congratulations. You know as well as I know that the lessons never stop. We are all students of life until the lights go out on us.)

I want to help you become a better, richer person regardless of how well or how poor you are currently living. This book is about maximizing your talents and dreams so you can transform your life into a winning game. That may sound like an overpromising declaration to make, but bear with me. I believe that part of my calling—part of the reason I was put on this Earth—was to make other people successful. But it's not always easy. Sometimes I feel like I'm on one side of the table and my audience is on the other. I hate watching a room full of frustration as people ponder their lives and seek a drinking fountain that promises wealth and achievement. I wish I could roll in that fountain and let people pour themselves a magical cup. But what fun would that be? It's gratifying and exhilarating to go after your dreams and work at them day in and day out—including the setbacks that reboot our systems from time to time and compel us to stop, self-examine, and reevaluate.

So I write this with a goal of becoming your motivator and teacher; I want you to feel like you've got me sitting by your side as you navigate what's potentially holding you back from getting all you want out of life. And please try to keep me on the same plane as you are on. Don't regard me as someone above you—someone who's out of your league because you look at me as rich in some distorted, literal definition of the word. If you really know me, then you know that I'd rather be rich in spirit than rich in monetary value. I just happen to have both at a young age. How? If a voice inside you said "because Farrah's a lucky guy," then this book is definitely for you. I'm going to dispel the erroneous connection we make with success and chance. With success and connections. With success and IQ. And even with success and money.

Before we go too deep, I want to be clear on the difference between being rich and being wealthy. Those words are thrown around in the same circles, but they are not the same. When someone says he is rich, what immediately comes to mind? Probably a big bank account with millions of dollars sitting in it. On the other hand, when someone says he is wealthy, does that word trigger a slightly different picture? Do you think about not only cash in the bank, but also homes, stocks, bonds, income properties, and so on? In other words, assets. Rich has a very in-the-moment and short-lived feeling to it. People get rich hitting the jackpot in Vegas or winning the lottery. Wealthy, on the other hand, equates with long-term success and a state of well-being that accompanies happiness and stability. It's the true combo of affluence and influence—concepts you'll learn about in this book. That said, I'm going to continue to use the word *rich*, because I want to guide you to a place where you adopt an entirely new meaning to this word.

By now you should have a clue that this isn't a get-rich-quick book, but I will be giving you tips that have worked for me on my journey to financial freedom. This is about getting real about what lies or myths you've come to believe and that continue to blind you from seeing that path to prosperity. Which is why you have to get real before you can get rich. If you still don't understand what I mean by the word *rich*, don't panic. You will by the end of this book. There's a high volume of gimmicky get-rich propaganda out there, so you have to move past *that* myth to see the real truth behind what it means to be rich. In my world, to be rich is to be more than wealthy—it entails having a financial, emotional, and spiritual sense of security. You can be rich whether you're making $20,000 a year or $2 million a year.

I got to where I am today by starting with one simple act that we all have the ability to perform. Do you know what that was? I made the decision to be prosperous in all facets of my life, and I'm happy to report that I'm living my dream. That's all it took— a decision. Well, okay, so there are some other things to know and do, all of which I'll be sharing with you. But it starts with a commitment to yourself. I'm confident that you can at least do that! And, since you've picked up this book, I'll give you credit for making half of that decision. The other half will happen soon, if it hasn't already.

I know what it has taken for me on my journey, and if you read my first book, *Reallionaire*, you're already familiar with my story. I grew up in the projects of Chicago's South Side with my brothers and sister. Given the statistics that said I'd probably be dead or in jail before I reached adulthood, you could say I was born to lose. Mother worked double, sometimes triple jobs to make ends meet. By the time I was six, I had decided it was time to help my family achieve a better standard of living. That's when I resolved to do whatever it took to beat the odds and win. No, I wasn't struck by lightning, and no one put a computer chip in my brain one night to make me successful. If anything, I had: 1) an acute awareness of my surroundings, and 2) the drive to change them. I've gotten used to people saying it's unusual to have such an awareness and ambition at a tender age, but it doesn't make a difference. See if you can take age out of the equation; I don't care (and neither should you) whether you're six or sixty-six. You can change at any age—and continue to do so. I believe we should follow our intuition and heart because they truly know where we want to be in life. We all are born with both heart and intuition.

I went door to door selling homemade body lotion and bookends I crafted from hand-painted rocks. By the age of seven I carried a business card that read 21ST CENTURY CEO, and I was hell-bent on seeing that dream come true. I latched on to a mentor and at age eight cofounded my first business, called the Urban Neighborhood Economic Enterprise Club (UNEEC). This was the forerunner of New Early Entrepreneur Wonders (NE2W), which later became the flagship organization I opened on Wall Street. By then I was fourteen and I had made history as the youngest person to have an office on the Street. NE2W enlisted, educated, and engaged at-risk youth by creating and developing legal ways for them to acquire additional income.

Right about now you're wondering, How'd he do it? How'd he get the money? Someone must have sponsored him. Someone must have paved the way for him to be so lucky and keep going. (Did you catch that? There's that word again: lucky. I know it passed through your mind again. Don't beat yourself up; you'll soon understand why twisted notions of luck come naturally today, and I'll help you get rid of them.)

"Keep going" is exactly what I did. But my journey had less to do with money and help from others and more to do with my attitude, my developing skills, and my commitment. You're going to hear those words a lot in this book: *attitude*, *skills*, and *commitment*. Because if there is ever a recipe for success that has nothing to do with external forces or luck, it entails those three key words.

I continued to found and operate lucrative businesses while getting involved in all sorts of ventures and media outlets. Like any successful human, I experienced disappointments along the way and had to overcome obstacles. But overall the series of decisions I made cultivated enough home runs for me to claim victory again and again. When I discovered Farr-Out Foods and created a tasty strawberry-vanilla syrup, for example, I suddenly found myself taking orders exceeding $1.5 million annually. It was time to sell. It was also the moment I realized that this success business wasn't rocket science. And I wanted to share my advice and inspiration with as many others as possible. This may sound implausible, but by the end of this book I will have proved the following to you: Everyone has an innate power to be successful, but not everyone is willing to do the work to harness that power (hence the statement I made at the very beginning). If you think you need a guide or step-by-step plan of action, then let this be your starting point.

This book takes the mysticism out of success. As long as we think success is a result of luck, chance, or magic, the rich get richer and the poor get poorer. As I grew up in a family that lacked in monetary wealth but was rich in spirit, I began a process of personal discovery to find out what makes one person succeed while another person fails. My findings were too exciting to keep to myself! My first book was largely autobiographical. It told my rags-to-riches story and offered some general exercises readers could do to apply the lessons gleaned from my own experience. But it wasn't enough; I know that you need more than that. Psychological "you can do it" is one thing, but having the tools to apply sound strategy in real life is clearly another. Let me give you an example.

You know you have to eat to stay alive; I don't have to inspire you to do that. But you may not know exactly what to eat—what foods to put in your mouth to optimize your health and longevity. The same holds true when offering advice on success. You need a strategy. You need some hand holding. It's like getting into a car—even though the mind provides a powerful navigation system (if not *the* most powerful!), we still prefer to have a point-to-point map. We want confirmation that taking a left turn here is okay. We also need a destination. Not many people would be willing to start driving if they didn't know where they were going. But how bad could that be? Have you ever gone for a drive with no set course or final destination in mind, and had a glorious time nonetheless? That's what life should be like. Unfortunately, people *think* they need an actual guide to live by. They seek structure, a reliable plan, an accurate road map. They need to know if they do this, then things will be okay. And that they will be successful.

Which brings me back to the reason I wrote this book. I am going to show you what I believe prevents you from your greatest achievement. And I'm going to take you by the hand and give you that map you think you need. Even though I likely will tell you what you already know somewhere deep inside, I will have ushered you through a mental process that hopefully will expunge whatever haunts your path to riches. Success is an inside job. If you cut your finger, the cut on your hand will heal itself—you don't have to command it to heal. The same is true of success. It's within all of us.

I encourage you to mark the page where you have your aha moment. May you have many of them! And I'll answer your most burning questions. You see, since the publication of *Reallionaire*, I've experienced changes in myself and I've witnessed shifts in our communities and the world at large. People who approach me today have questions that I've never heard before, and that hadn't been relevant until now, as a result of evolving technology and changes in our economic and business climates. From broad perspectives on the rules to financial well-being to specific advice on prioritizing types of investments, for example, I'll provide insights on how you can plan for making more money in the future and raising your income today. I'll also offer tips on effective problem solving and how to keep your character in shape so that taking action will be easy and comfortable.

There's no shortage of inspirational books out there, just as there's no shortage of books that can teach you how to do X or Y or Z. Consider all the *Dummies* and *Idiot's* guides. Every bookstore has a how-to section. Self-help gurus from every department (health, finance, spiritual, and so on) are plentiful. But obviously there's a disconnect between the wisdom of how to take the proper action and the confidence and motivation to do so—a disconnect this book attempts to bridge. I find most people simply don't know what it is they are supposed to be doing.

They are not happy with their current jobs, but they don't know how to get out of them, either. Just quit! But you might want to wait until Friday. In life we reserve the right to make decisions. Here's what I think: Nobody forced you to work the job that you hate. That's a decision you made. You decided to get up and get dressed today, right? Yes, these are slightly obnoxious questions and statements, because of course you are compelled to get up and go to work. You have rent or a mortgage to pay and a family to feed. My point is that you have the power of choice. And it is with this exact same power of choice that you can change your life and choose to be successful.

Let's return to that car analogy for a moment. If I gave you a set of keys to a car (any car you like), could you hop in and find your destination? I know, you'd want me to tell you where to go. Like I said, there's no shortage of maps and guides (or GPS gadgets) to get you anywhere. But there definitely is a lack of personalized instructions on how to find *your* specific destination— the place you're *supposed* to go to and stand tall.

There's a clear reason why this book is structured around seven lies. When I sat down to figure out how I could best articulate my message and lessons to maximally contribute to your dreams and future, I couldn't get these myths—these lies that pervade our culture—out of my head. They are what I am up against every time I speak in front of an audience full of restless, fearful people who have trouble believing they can be whatever they want to be. These seven fallacies represent the biggest inhibitors to achievement in the general population; those who reject them and embrace their truths are those top 1 percent of people whom you'd call successful. And you can be one of them.

We live in a world driven by money and ideals, but most notably by fears. Fear of change, fear of taking risks, fear of losing, fear of failure. Fear is why we can easily cling to false beliefs and let them control our way of thinking. For example, if I were to ask you if you thought it was possible to have both debt and wealth, the latter being predominant, what would you say? (You can be the difference in making it into the top 1 percent.) Must you have an understanding of stocks and bonds to be rich? Is there an action plan with a high probability of success that doesn't entail a brainy degree or a wild invention? What are the secrets to making more money right this second? I will answer all these questions plus more. Their answers may surprise you.

Too many of us live paycheck to paycheck and pray that those compilations of books and CDs and DVDs somehow will lead us to automatic wealth. News flash: There's no such thing as automatic wealth—at least not in the real world. Of course some people will have you believe that wealth starts with a way of thinking and then moves effortlessly toward real wealth. In this book I challenge you to move beyond the conversation and really grab at your accomplishments. I'm not only going to share the mind-set you need to achieve all that you dream of, but also the specific strategies that accompany that state of mind. I want to help you marshal out your own wealth potential, which relates to everything about you—not just your bank account. You might be oblivious to the fears and fallacies that are thwarting you financially, spiritually, emotionally, and even physically. I'm a strong believer that what happens in your personal world will show up in your professional world, so you must always maintain a healthy balance and live fearlessly . . . from the inside out. You'll soon come to know what I mean, and no matter what your age is it will change your life.

When my nine-year-old goddaughter saw me speak a while back, she went through an exercise I'll have you do in Chapter 2. It got her to see what it was she should be focusing on, which was writing. She then made the decision to put her efforts into practicing her craft, and guess what. She landed a book deal with Poetry .com to be a contributing author, beating out more than 100,000 other people in the same contest. Not bad for a nine-year-old.

I had my own epiphany when I was nine years old. It was listening to Nelson Mandela's inaugural speech, which motivated me to continue to live without fear at all times:

> Our deepest fear is not that we are inadequate. Our deepest fear is that we are powerful beyond measure. It is our light, not our darkness that most frightens us. We ask ourselves, who am I to be brilliant, gorgeous, talented, and fabulous? Actually, who are you not to be? You are a child of God. Your playing small does not serve the world. There is nothing enlightened about shrinking so that other people won't feel insecure around you. We are all meant to shine, as children do. We were born to make manifest the glory of God that is within us. It's not just in some of us; it's in everyone. And as we let our own light shine, we unconsciously give other people permission to do the same. As we are liberated from our own fear, our presence automatically liberates others.

Now I ask you, *What's holding you back*? The answer to that question is what this book is about. What is it about your way of thinking and the choices you've made that have gotten you to this point in your life? What do you want to change? And how will you go about stamping out fear and executing that change? Keep those questions in mind as you read through this book. I'll be asking them again a bit later on.

Are you ready to live fearlessly? Hop in that metaphorical car of your choice and let your journey begin.

1

The Born-Lucky Lie

Lie: I have to be born with connections or a special talent to be rich.

Truth: Luck is showing up. You can't win if you don't play.

Lucky shirts, lucky jackets, lucky underwear. Back in the day, people always talked about the rabbit's foot. They had to have one on their key chain for good luck. Here's what I have to say about that: The rabbit had *four* feet . . . and he still got killed.

Luck is someone doing something, pure and simple. The operative word here is, of course, *something*. It's about taking action, which this book is going to show you how to do. By most definitions of the word, luck entails chance. Do you want to leave your ability to get rich to chance? What if you're not a *chosen* one? Then what? Take a deep breath. Don't panic. Luck has nothing to do with prosperity. You will succeed if *you* choose to.

When we hear about someone's fame and fortune, it's not hard to automatically think, "Yeah, well, look at who his *father* is, or . . . look at where she went to *school*, or . . . look at the *talent* God gave him, making it relatively easy to strike it rich. I don't have that kind of luck."

This is the born-lucky lie, and it's one of the most pervasive myths out there that stops people dead in their tracks. Not only does it blind you from visualizing your own potential, but it also prevents you from realizing that potential—going out toward your destiny and reaching your own highest peak. Lots of people are born into privilege but go absolutely nowhere. Those who choose to use their talents—and I believe everybody has them—can do great things regardless of where or under what circumstances they were born.

WHAT IS LUCK?

People who complain that they don't have what it takes to be wealthy because they lack something like connections, an inheritance, a trust fund, or a talent are fooling themselves. You're giving in to this lie if you think that's true.

Luck is an everyday word. We hear it so often that it's nearly impossible to see it for what it is: a total sham. It's been branded by popular companies, and even Google offers an "I'm feeling lucky" button on its main search engine site. No wonder so many people fall prey to its deceits. Successful people talk more about dedicated work than luck. But people continue to mistake it for success. I ask you, does luck guide the tennis swing of Serena?

Can luck make a poor person just wake up one day and have the riches of Bill Gates? Can luck make a blind person see? I don't think so. And also consider this: The vast majority of *Inc.* 500 leaders come from middle class, lower class, or poor backgrounds. Was it luck that got them there? Or was it a mixture of lots of other, more profound, and concrete things like drive, ambition, and hustle? I'd say the latter.

Samuel Goldwyn (the "G" of the MGM studios empire) once said, "The harder I work, the luckier I get." With all due respect to Mr. Goldwyn, I have trouble with that statement. In fact, the quote moved me when I first heard it, not because I found it inspiring but because it made me wince. I don't believe it. I wish Samuel Goldwyn were alive today so I could storm his Hollywood office and get him to admit that his so-called luck wasn't luck at all. It was his passion, skills, and foresight. It was his courage to be authentic and go after his dreams. And it was his ability to seize opportunities when they emerged. He'd probably agree with me. He'd probably also agree with how I define hard work, which we'll be getting to shortly.

Of course, we could be walking a fine line here that boils down to semantics. What Samuel Goldwyn calls luck may very well be his version of saying, "My interests and ambitions allowed me to accomplish a lot." But let's be real—when most people think of the word *luck*, they relate it to getting something for nothing. They view luck as a magical phenomenon that strikes when it wants to, and is not under anyone's control. So if you're lucky, you were in the right place at the right time.

> **REALITY CHECK**: Who determines what's the right place at the right time? Luck? And what does luck look like, so we know when we've found it? Only *you* can show up at the right time and the right place. Luck has nothing to do with it, because it doesn't exist. No one is born lucky. By the way, I believe the concept of being "at the right place at the right time" is a complete and utter falsehood.

Let's go back to Mr. Goldwyn. Here's a man who certainly wasn't born lucky by any stretch of that word. He came into the world named Schmuel Gelbfisz in Warsaw, Poland, to an impoverished Jewish family in 1882. At an early age he left home penniless and on foot, eventually making his way to England, where he stayed with relatives for a few years. He then emigrated to the United States, landing in New York City in 1899. No sooner did he get into the garment business than he realized he had an innate skill for marketing. He could sell anything, and he became a very successful salesman. When he discovered that he had a love for film—at that time the industry was in its infancy—the combination of his astute salesmanship and passion for movies eventually led him to Hollywood, where he developed into a legendary motion picture producer and founder of several studios. Luck? Most certainly not. Goldwyn was someone who tapped his talent and who merely who showed up . . . a lot. Which brings me to the first truth:

THE BORN-LUCKY TRUTH

Luck is **showing up.**
You can't win if you don't play.

GOOD WORK, NOT GOOD LUCK

Notice that I said Mr. Goldwyn *developed* into a successful entertainment mogul. From the get-go I want to be clear: Successful people, including individual small-business owners, are *developed*—not born. They evolve over time, continually learning and honing their skills and seeking new opportunities to further polish their abilities. Where do they start? Often with the help of at least one other person, such as a friend or family member who acts as a sounding board for their ideas and interests. For Goldwyn, that person was a man by the name of Jesse Lasky, a vaudeville performer who was also his brother-in-law. Together they hooked up with a theater owner, Adolph Zukor, and produced their first film, using an ambitious young director named Cecil B. DeMille. The rest is history.

Everyone needs a confidant and a positive mentor in life, regardless of age. Besides my own momma and grandma, another special person profoundly affected my way of thinking at an early age. When he entered my life he essentially became my first mentor outside my home, and he was to shape the path I'd take in business. I owe a great deal of thanks to this man for setting my mind right regarding the notion of luck before it really brainwashed me. If you read my first book, you already may be familiar with Roi Tauer, who operated a Chicago-based think tank. He played a big part in getting my first business endeavor up and running. He was my persistent teacher, instructing me on the steps to take and challenging me along the way to clean out the stereotypes and false ideas I had rolling around my head. At the time I'd been around so much poverty and depravity that thinking about money was like having an allergy I couldn't shake loose. I saw it as the ultimate destination, and that the means to that end was pure luck.

Good work, not good luck were Roi's words to me. He made me repeat that phrase over and over again. It didn't stick until he asked, Who is Farrah? What are his strengths and weaknesses? How well does he fight? Are his mind, body, and spirit in good shape? Most of these questions were a bit sophisticated for me; after all, I was only eight years old (and I took the word *fight* literally at first). But when I let them sink in, they eventually had a huge effect on me. I realized I could take control of my life. That it was up to me to do the work. And that if there was anything true about luck, it was all in the mind.

While I salute Roi for helping me nourish the seeds of my business mind at an early age, I must pay tribute to my grandma, who instilled in me so much about winning in life. When I was seven I had a teacher tell me that I'd amount to nothing. According to her, I was living in poverty and I'd stay in poverty. The statistics said I'd be in jail or dead by my teenage years, so there was nowhere for me to go (but jail or six feet under). I dashed home and shared this with my grandma. She set me straight, telling me that everyone puts his pants on one leg at a time in the morning, unless he jumps into them. She told me to wake up every morning and ask myself, *Why not me?* Which is exactly what I did that next morning, and every morning thereafter.

We forget to ask ourselves that question, especially when faced by others who judge us. Can you find a reason why another person has done something and not you? We often give our power away. To other people. To opinions. To fears. To falsities. To this warped perception of luck. Most people live their fears, not their possibilities. Considering the fact that we only use a small percentage of our brain, why not try to utilize more of it and work on expanding it? It's amazing what you can accomplish when you don't know what you can't do yet. God didn't take a nap on the day you were born. We are all blessed and gifted, but it's how we recognize those blessings and gifts that allows us to go to a higher level.

So with the influence of my grandma affecting my thinking, little revelations led me to understand what makes a person rich. Rich wasn't about money per se or the amount of luck one had in life. No, being rich was so much more.

WHAT IT MEANS TO BE RICH

Mark G. is a man who typifies the person who *doesn't* know what it means to be rich. I bet you know someone like Mark. He talks incessantly about money and dreams of a big payday in the future but isn't doing much to cultivate his talents and passions today. He works a 9 to 5 job he hates, and he doesn't care that he owes people money, because he proclaims he's going to be rich someday. Just wait, he'll be winning the world over soon . . .

When I pose those same questions I got as a kid, like "Who is Mark? What are you here on Earth to do? What makes you special?" I don't get much of a response. I sense that his self-esteem is on the low side because when I encourage him to tell me what he wants to do in life, presumably to achieve his giant payday, he says he's "saving himself for that one thing that will make him somebody." He believes it will rescue him and bring him to the place he's been dreaming about, which is also vague and indescribable. But he has no idea what that one thing will be. In short, he's busy not knowing what it takes to get there. And he has no idea what to do with himself but wait, as if luck will strike at random when he least expects it.

There is only one true road to real success. A mirage lies at the end of that other road I unfortunately see too many take. That's the one where you fantasize about prosperity, waiting and hoping, but you do zilch to further a goal or work on yourself as a person. You likely think that high self-esteem will magically turn up the day you hit it big, too.

The real road, on the other hand, is working on raising your self-esteem each and every day so when you *do* experience success, you're ready for it and are much less likely to fail. Even if you're not exactly sure right now what your purpose in life is, at least you can start devoting more time to exploring your talents and building more self-confidence. This will then help you to figure out your real purpose.

REALITY CHECK: How well do you know yourself? Are you moving closer to or further from your goals in life? Start a journal today that records your hopes, dreams, thoughts, values, and even frustrations and disappointments.

You may choose to break up the journal into two sections—one that is sectioned off by the chapters in this book with its related exercises, and one that's devoted for special sections. Write your name on the cover and be proud of it. Ask your parents what it means or how they arrived at that name for you if you don't know already. (My name means "burden bearer" in Arabic—the one who carries great responsibility. No wonder I was destined to lead, set examples, and inspire. It's not a burden, however. It's a blessing and an honor.) Set aside a special section for affirmations, favorite quotes, or poems (look up "Equipment" by Edgar A. Guest; it's one of my favorite poems), as well as a section for keeping track of mentors, contacts, and the relationships you will make to further your goals and dreams. You may also want to save space for including notes that emerge from important conversations. I also recommend a section devoted to your ideas. This is where you can have a conversation with yourself on paper and flesh out possibilities. Seeing your ideas written down can offer clarity, or convince you to keep testing new ideas.

MONEY DOESN'T MAKE HAPPINESS GO 'ROUND

Money changes people, *sort of*. I think we all know someone who would be dangerous around a sudden windfall of cash. The worst thing that could happen to this person *is* money, the reason being that they will rush out and buy copious unnecessary items to fill up the void that is their soul. Hit the jackpot today, hit the mall tomorrow. I once met a woman who was so caught up in brands and the image of wealth that the moment she came into some money, she announced she was dashing out to buy some "Escader," "Christian Dinor-ah," "Lewis Vitton," and "Prader." Clearly she wasn't able even to pronounce the brands, but now she could buy them all and load up her closets, masking a low self-esteem in her personal house. The money wouldn't help fill up her spiritual bank, her mind and soul. I was saddened by how she talked, but when I tried to explain to her that the material goods wouldn't make her happy and satisfied in the end, she wasn't ready to listen.

Which brings me to an important detail. The fact that you are reading this book means you are ready to hear the message. A voice inside your head is telling you that it's time to make a change. You are ready to get real, and get rich. For some, hearing what I have to say about certain things may make you uncomfortable. I may suggest something that goes so strongly against conventional wisdom and your deepest-held beliefs that you may want to close the book and calm down a bit. I don't care what you think or don't think about what it takes to be rich. My hope is that you learn to dispel at least a few of these lies and learn how to turn my message into action. Remember, a car can be supplied and gassed up to the max, but it still won't go anywhere if someone doesn't start the engine and press the accelerator.

Getting real is about getting aligned with yourself first and foremost. You can't get rich unless you come into who you are, your purpose, and then build your richness from the inside out. We see many celebrities fall from grace when they get a taste of success but don't have a solid foundation—a grounding rooted in a deep knowing of themselves—to support their continued prosperity. I don't even care to give names. The tabloids say it all.

Some people are driven by money. But let's face it: Money isn't hard to make—assassins, prostitutes, and drug dealers make money. You don't need to be lucky to make money. People confuse luck with money. At the end of the day, you have to ask yourself what kind of pillow you want to sleep on and how well you want to sleep at night. I've seen many people walk away from loads of money for this simple reason: They just weren't happy. All the money in the world can't buy confidence and self-esteem. It may be human nature to think the grass is greener on the other side and that money can make a difference. I'm going to show you otherwise.

It's been argued that $50,000 is the income level above which there's a law of diminishing returns on the happiness meter. More money doesn't beget more happiness. While it's been shown that money buys more happiness when it moves you out of poverty and into the middle class, money loses its purchasing power quickly once you reach $50,000. In other words, there's an enormous difference in the level of happiness between earning

$10,000 or $50,000 but an insignificant difference between earning $100,000 and $1 million. In the transition between poverty and middle class, the money is buying you out of poor health, adversity, worrying about where your next meal will come from, and stressing about your children's future and safety. When those essential needs are satisfied, what's left?

Dr. Daniel Gilbert, a psychologist at Harvard, uses a great analogy: One stack of pancakes tastes delicious. The second starts to lose its lusciousness. If you force-feed a third stack of rich, heavy pancakes down, it gets uncomfortable. More pancakes don't equate with more satisfaction. Sound familiar? Well, the same holds true with money. Even people who rake in six- or seven-figure salaries can live paycheck to paycheck. What happens is they elevate their living standards when their income goes up, so even though they may be making more money, they still live above their means and still dream of the day they won't have to worry about money and be unhappy about themselves.

Dr. Gilbert has studied and written a lot about happiness. He asserts that the reason we often are so bad at predicting what will make us happy is because we are prone to *illusions of our imagination*. It's the same thing as being prone to illusions of memory and perception. We don't realize how much imagination puts in and leaves out, how much the imagined future is influenced by the actual present, and how differently we will think about the future once it happens. This is also the case when it comes to money matters. What we think of as being rich is merely an illusion, and we easily can fall prey to the illusion that money will make us happy, "big," confident, and well-respected. In a word, rich.

Well, I'm here to tell you point-blank that the money won't make you; you need to make the money. The happy, grand chicken comes before the egg in this game. The richest people in the world who are also happy lay golden eggs because they've worked on their personal character and self-esteem long before they were ready to count chickens.

> REALITY CHECK: Being rich *is* being happy. Being rich is about knowing who you are and using your talents to the best of your abilities.

Being rich is having high self-esteem, which doesn't include ego and arrogance. Contrary to popular belief, high achievers are extremely humble. They don't have self-esteem issues, because they work on themselves every day through their accomplishments, both big and small. They are secure in their dreams and understand the value of achievement. With every little success they have, they gain confidence. Nothing is taken for granted or assumed to be handed over on a silver platter. An arrogant person, on the other hand, is coming from a place of lack. He's traveling on the road to the mirage. Whenever I encounter an arrogant person, I think, "Who died and made you God? *I missed that meeting.*"

BE YOUR OWN CHEERLEADER

So what can you do today with your current income to make a positive change? Before we get to the business of making more money, we first have to start by having more positive conversations with ourselves. There is a lot of power in affirmations because words can be extremely commanding. They help to disarm the negativity that's a fact of life. We don't often have other people cheerleading us on and telling us what we'd like to hear on a daily basis. It's up to you to tell yourself those things. I encourage you to wake up every morning, look into the mirror, and say all the nice things you wish someone else would tell you. Self-affirmation is as simple as telling yourself "I can!" Go crazy and mix descriptive affirmations with forward-thinking phrases: "I'm intelligent. I'm creative. I'm successful. I will prosper. I'm beautiful. I'm ambitious. I will achieve my dreams. I'm worthy. I'm courageous. I will work at what I do best. I'm accountable and responsible for my own destiny. I'm fortunate. I'm blessed. I will preserve a healthy body. I'm spirited. I'm compassionate. I will be my own boss someday." Once *you* are convinced of these things, you can then convince *other* people, and the world will open up to your dreams.

If you don't look at yourself differently, you can't achieve anything different. In life we don't get what we want; we get what we *are*. You may be familiar with the theory that words influence our behaviors, which then become habits, and all of which lead to our destiny. I wholeheartedly believe in this theory. I think it's a reality. Positive words become positive behaviors and habits that then carry us to the destiny we so crave. If we stay caught up in the negative, we will arrive at a destiny we don't care for. A pianist can learn how to read and play music, but without physically practicing and keeping those fingers in shape for the keyboard, she can't play well and get through a tricky tarantella smoothly from memory. The same happens in life. Positive affirmation helps us keep our brains trained and in shape from a psychological perspective to think positively, which then affects our behaviors. If you can act in a way that effortlessly supports your dreams and goals, then that's what I call success.

> What you think about, you bring about.
>
> —OLD SAYING

I also encourage you to take time-outs during the day to use affirmations. We engage in too much negative conversation with ourselves: "Oh, you're so stupid. Oh, I'm always messing up. I've never gotten what I want. I don't deserve to be rich. I'll always be broke . . ." When we say these words, what they are communicating is "this will happen again." We are dooming ourselves before it even happens! Don't reflect on bad things that happened in the past. Let them go. Don't tell that story about when you were a kid; it's not happening anymore, so don't keep reliving it. Your memories and your future are very similar. When you think about something, you're actually living it—at that point in time. So whether you're thinking of your future or your past, you are bringing them into the present. And a compulsion to reflect on a past rife with troubles and disappointments won't help us move forward into a productive future. This is the danger of victim syndrome, which is when you are so hung up on past failures that you are left paralyzed. There's a difference between using mistakes as excuses and actually learning from them. Negative thoughts and feelings are disempowering. You can blame all of the bad people and bad experiences in your life for your shortcomings, but if you own up to your life and take responsibility for your destiny, you can empower yourself and make a difference in your future. Truly successful people are accountable for their own lives. They make the decision to be a member of the success world and use all that they know—past and present—to get there.

Words Can Be Stronger Than Actions

Words can quickly morph into habits and behaviors, so in a sense they are stronger than actions because they often come *first*. If you are feeding yourself negative words, especially ones based on frustrations about your past, you are going to engender negative behaviors now and in the future. Rather than doom yourself with negative thoughts, try owning up to what *has* happened instead of what *might* happen, and be done with it. If, for example, you are broke, tell yourself "Hey, it's unfortunate that I've been bad with money in the past, but now I'm going to be rich." The key word here is "past." It's over, so now you can move forward with that knowledge under your belt. See if you can accept the bad things in your past as lessons for a prosperous future.

Focus instead on a prosperous future, which you can then bring toward you in the present. Those daily affirmations will help you cultivate the winning attitude you need as your partner.

Here is a sampling of words you should strive to say about yourself:

Affectionate	Friendly	Playful
Ambitious	Fulfilled	Positive
Amusing	Funny	Powerful
Artistic	Generous	Practical
Balanced	Gracious	Productive
Blessed	Graceful	Progressive
Caring	Happy	Prosperous
Charismatic	Healthy	Realistic
Committed	Honest	Resilient
Compassionate	Humble	Responsible
Considerate	Insightful	Rich
Courageous	Inspiring	Sensitive
Creative	Meticulous	Sociable
Dedicated	Mindful	Spirited
Determined	Modest	Strong
Direct	Organized	Successful
Driven	Outgoing	Sympathetic
Empowering	Passionate	Systematic
Energetic	Patient	Tenacious
Fortunate	Persistent	Wise
Free	Persuasive	Worthy

Take note of the words you don't think apply to you right now, and don't be afraid to add others. We often define ourselves by what we *do* rather than who we are. But it's what we *are* that defines what and how well we do. Is a comedian great because he is funny or is he funny because he is a comedian? Considering the words that describe you best and least will help you come to understand yourself better and give you some things to think about as you move forward and align your true self with your true calling. My hope is that you can match the vision you have for yourself with your true vision—the one God intended you to have. Ask yourself which words you want to claim as belonging to you.

I recently had a conversation with a woman who had this type of counterproductive attitude and victim mentality. She was applying to a graphic-design program but still sucking on life's lemons, complaining about her past failures. Then she concluded, "I can't do it. Even my family says I can't do this. What am I thinking?"

I said to her, "You're thinking like a loser. In fact, you've already lost because you've called the game. You won't win unless you change your mind about whose side you're playing on. Can you be your own cheerleader? Can you be on your own side? Everyone is telling you what you can't do, including you. Whose side are you on? Yours or theirs? Can you at least be the only person on your side?"

She started laughing and said, "You're right."

"There will be thousands of people in this world to doubt you. They don't need your help," I returned. For a moment she was transfixed on this last thought. Then she smiled.

SEND "THEY" PACKING

Okay, so I know that turning off negative conversation is easier said than done. You have to literally say "Stop it!" to yourself. We have upward of 60,000 thoughts a day (no wonder we can get exhausted so easily from thinking alone), and it's been argued that the vast majority of those thoughts are negative. No surprise there. But here's a thought: Who are you comparing yourself to all the time? Who sets the standards? Like the saying goes: "You know what they say . . ." Well, I ask you, who is "*they*"? We continually compare ourselves to the bogeyman—someone who doesn't exist. Who says you're not good enough? Smart enough? Pretty enough? I never met "they" before. Have you?

Much of what we do is like playing chess. I cheer on anybody who learns to play chess. In that game, you have to plan a move at least three moves in advance. If you can operate in life with that same mind-set, you have a powerful tool. If you're not thinking two or three steps ahead, you're not able to continue moving forward to rise above your current self. Centuries ago Aesop shared this moral in a fable called "The Ant and the Grasshopper." While the grasshopper spends the warm months singing, the ant works to store up food for winter. The ant is thinking three months in advance. After the winter arrives, the grasshopper finds itself dying of hunger, and upon asking the ant for food is only rebuked for its idleness. Thinking about what lies ahead and planning today is a virtue. You don't have to run like the hare, but you can be the tortoise who wins the slow and steady race of strategy. In the upcoming chapters you'll be learning strategies to guide you in your own personal race, regardless of who you're up against. You'll be sending all of those "theys" packing.

People ask me why I've never changed. They assume that my money would turn me into a different person, like it appears to do to so many others. (Notice I said *appears.*) I tell them that money doesn't change who you are at the core. Much to the contrary, it magnifies who you really are. So if your self-esteem is running low, guess what? The money will push your self-esteem even lower. You won't know what to do with the money, and it could destroy you. That's when you discover the bitter, harsh truth that money doesn't make you special. You're still the same old person. A better idea would be to work on the person that would be left if everything were to be taken away from you. That's what I bear in mind every day. It keeps me grounded. It keeps me on the path of prosperity. And it keeps me real.

You are to make the money; the money doesn't make you.

MOVE BEYOND THE LOTTERY MENTALITY

The time has come to evict luck from our vocabulary. As I mentioned, some people think that if they just wake up, they will become successful and make it big. We all have someone in our lives who sits around talking about their future payday. They are "saving" themselves for that single moment when they win the Lotto or when a deal falls into their lap, or they are waiting on some other dream of success, which never comes, of course, because there is no action taken. While they are in their holding pattern wishing on a star for good luck, they never bother with good work.

I'll admit that some people seem to live charmed lives, with money and opportunities constantly falling into their laps. But I don't know any of those people, and chances are you don't, either. If someone comes to mind, please tell me. And make sure you ask him or her if luck or sheer dedication is to be credited. Ask how many puddles and pitfalls they had to endure in their journey.

I believe that successes and failures come into our lives based on choices we make. You can have a great influence over the major events in your life by making plans and working toward specific goals. Choice is so much more important than luck. You have to choose to take action. You have to choose to cause money to show up in your life. When you watch a flower bloom in your garden, you can trace the cause back to the seeds you planted, the water you gave it, and the spot where you positioned it perfectly in the sunlight. Just as the choices you made in caring for the flower allow it to grow and thrive, the choices you make in life are what determine your future—whether you will thrive or wilt.

Let's take a more serious example and look at poverty. Why are people poor? Do you believe that poor people were destined to be poor? Or that it's just the way of the world that some people will be poor and some will be rich? I believe eternal poverty is a choice, not a sentence.

> **REALITY CHECK:** You have to move beyond the lottery mentality, which is believing in luck or that something great can come from no effort.

Even the person who wins the lottery still had to put forth effort of *some* sort—get up, take a shower, get dressed, and go to a place where lottery tickets are sold. He has to pay for a ticket, and pay for a chance. The odds, however, are against him. It's harder to win the lottery than it is to be successful. You can't control the picking of the winning numbers, the "luck."

Like me, you may not have been born into the richest of households, but you don't have to accept that scenario for yourself. You see, barring any serious emotional or mental challenges, we all have the brainpower to get out of a dire financial situation. Sometimes the choices we make with our money lead us down a trail of struggle, bad credit, and paucity. In this case, it's the result of a failure to plan for success. The good news is that you can do it differently by making different plans for a different outcome. Once you realize that your life is a do-it-yourself project the options become exciting.

But you can control how much effort you put into working toward prosperity. The more effort you put forward, the better chance you have at becoming wealthy. If you were to ask a millionaire how much effort she put into becoming rich, I bet she would say "a lot." The funny part is that luck is elusive and it takes more time to wait for it than to simply create a plan and work it. Step out of your comfort zone and push yourself.

Here's a thought: The harder you work, the luckier you *are*. That's how Mr. Goldwyn should have put it. No one "gets" luck, as if it falls randomly from the sky. You *are* luck when you build a fortune from inner integrity and impassioned work.

THE IMPERSONAL UNIVERSE

As you begin to make changes in your life, you'll need to understand that the universe is impersonal. It doesn't care how rich, smart, privileged, or pretty you are. If you walk off a building, you will plummet downward. Gravity works on everybody. It doesn't discriminate. When you were a baby, you were not aware of the laws that govern electricity. If you wet your hand and stuck it into a socket, *bam*! You learned your lesson. But the law of electricity still exists, and even though you choose not to play with sockets anymore, you know what could happen if you did. Again, the universe is impersonal. So how does this apply to success?

If you think you're talented, guess what? The world doesn't care. It won't reward you automatically or bestow on you what you want. Like I said at the beginning, the world is full of talented people who amount to nothing. What matters is drive, determination, and hustle—concepts you're going to hear about repeatedly in this book. There are eight days a week when you have *drive*. There's a fire in your belly and you can't sleep well when you've got *passion* for your aspirations. And doing something everyone thinks cannot be done is a sign of *hustle*.

The problem is that people often don't show up. They don't show up for their relationships, for their jobs, for their passions. They let life lead them rather than take control of their lives. And they act confused when they are unhappy and "unlucky." If you work on finding your area of excellence, which is what we're going to do in the next chapter, then you will begin to see how luck doesn't really exist. And you'll be motivated to show up for success.

GET READY TO SHOW UP FOR SUCCESS

Success is about the law of averages. You have to increase the number of opportunities you have to meet people, establish a network, open more doors. I think it's sad that so many people today want things to happen to them; they don't want to put much work in getting to where they *think* they want to be. But a successful person is simply someone who showed up and did something, usually something no one else could do as well. When we admire or grow jealous of someone who has it all, someone we're likely to call lucky, we forget to look at ourselves and figure out how to better show up. The person who has achieved a lot simply knows how to show up, and you can, too.

Whether you're looking to meet a soul mate or start a company, you can't do it from the comforts of home. You can't get a date without getting visible. You can't jump-start a company without customers and clients. You have to get out there and leave the comfort zone—today. You'll hear me say this time and time again: Comfort is the enemy of achievement. The key to success is in the numbers: how many times you attempt something, how many times you have to hear a no before a yes; how many times you have to go back to the drawing board and find a new direction; how many times you have to reinvent yourself and start new conversations.

Jennifer Hudson provides a great case in point. Here's a Cinderella lady who turned disappointment into success. In 2004 she earned minor attention as one of the twelve finalists on the third season of the popular *American Idol* talent search show. With no formal musical training to speak of, she managed to wow *Idol* judges, and rumor had it she'd be one of three powerhouse finalists alongside the singers Fantasia Barrino and LaToya London. But rumor also had it that viewers didn't like her. She was a plus-size woman with a distinct musical style that, many argued, didn't jibe with the show's image. Rather than gain more time in the spotlight, she was unceremoniously whittled out of the pack. Fantasia stole the show and won the competition.

But Jennifer's fifteen minutes of fame didn't run out. She dipped into obscurity for two years, performing on the road and presumably working on herself and her music. Then she found her way into the auditioning room of the long-awaited film version of the Broadway musical *Dreamgirls* for the coveted role of Effie Melody White, the cast-off member of the sixties Supremes-like girl group. Among Jennifer's competition of over 750 hopefuls was Fantasia herself. But this time Jennifer was the winner, and she was even instructed to gain weight for the role. With the task of stepping up to a role so closely identified with Tony-winning legend Jennifer Holliday on Broadway, the making of *Dreamgirls* for Jennifer Hudson could only have been described as daunting, surreal, and thrilling. Indeed, she was daunted, but she still showed up to play.

It was a make-or-break role of a lifetime, and she nailed it on the head. Soon after the movie landed in theaters in 2006, the accolades started to roll in. Hudson quickly became the iconic symbol of the film's heart and soul, outshining even the esteemed Beyoncé Knowles and Eddie Murphy. She earned countless awards, from a New York Film Critics Circle Award and Golden Globe, to the British Academy Film Award and, finally, the coveted Oscar itself to complete the fairy-tale ending. What if she hadn't show up for that *Dreamgirls* audition after losing on *Idol*? What if she hadn't worked on herself during the hiatus between *Idol* and *Dreamgirls*? No one dwells on her disappointing loss on *Idol*. Few recall her little tour that preceded that prophetic audition. Everyone, of course, has her performance on the big screen locked in memory. Proof again that luck is merely somebody doing something extraordinary.

Nothing beats a failure but a try.
Persistence overcomes resistance.

—OLD ADAGE

The more you show up for success, the greater the chance you have at succeeding—period. Moreover, you have to be willing to do the things today that others would put off for tomorrow. Only then will you have the results of the life you want tomorrow.

This brings me to another lie related to luck that I touched on earlier and want to crush again so I can share its truth. I'm talking about the "you have to be at the right place at the right time" lie. Who said that? There's not much autonomy in this suggestion. How can you foresee a "right place" at the "right time"? Sounds like another misinformed tribute to luck and its deceptions. Sounds like you're supposed to show up tomorrow empty-handed and someone magically will give you what you're seeking. Fat chance. Here's the truth: You have to be everywhere all the time, letting people know you exist. Show up prepared with the drive, ambition, and hustle. But don't let it overwhelm you.

Lie: You have to be at the right place at the right time.
Truth: You have to be everywhere all the time.

By now you know that I grew up poor. I had to walk a long way to see nice things—about forty blocks total to and from home, which, when I consider that in miles, had to be more than a couple. My brother and I would sing as we walked to take our minds off the distance. It sure seemed to get us to our destination a lot sooner. Instead of getting caught up in the physical journey, we found ways to entertain ourselves, especially on the way back home when we were tired. But imagine if we thought about having to walk forty blocks at the start. We wouldn't have en-joyed it, and maybe we would have bailed on the whole trip.

It's important not to look at the journey as exhausting. Don't think about how long it will take or how tiring it might be. Just focus on taking those steps one after the other and enjoying the process. Thoughts can be exhausting. If you let your thoughts run wild, especially before you've even started, they can run you over pretty quickly and leave you too tired to do anything. Re-member, most of those thoughts tend to be negative. You know that nothing gets built in a day. After all, that's the purpose of time. To make sure nothing happens all at once.

Distances can be intimidating and set an ominous tone. But once something is behind us, the intimidation vanishes because we've already conquered it. When you get used to punking fear, you get over fear. When you are in the habit of facing your fears, you become fearless. How is this possible? Start with those affir-mations. In fact, before you move on to Chapter 2, put the book down and go stand in front of the mirror. Appreciate yourself and your strengths. At the end of every chapter I want you to see if you can put some of my advice into action before reading on. Take the best advice you find and entertain yourself by putting it into action.

So starting today, do at least one affirmation for thirty days straight. It takes that long to make anything a habit. At the end of thirty days, you'll feel better about yourself and better able to work on getting rich—rich in the way I want you to get rich. Financial wealth is relatively easy to achieve; it's the inner game of wealth that is more difficult to master, and that should come first.

Have you ever met Fear? Do you know him? What does he look like? Where does he live? News Flash: He's not an object, person, or thing. "He's" a fictional image you're chasing in your mind. Open any dictionary and look up the word *failure*. Somewhere buried among the false definitions is the true meaning of failure:

> *not doing; neglect or omission; nonperformance of a duty.*

DON'T GO IT ALONE

Just as nothing gets built in a day, self-made millionaires don't get made in a vacuum. I can't reiterate enough how important it is to find a mentor to guide you and be a source of advice and encouragement. In fact, three things I want you to be thinking about, starting today, are my ABCs for preparing yourself for success:

   a. A mentor and support group
   b. A willingness to get uncomfortable
   c. A winning attitude

Find and Mind the Mentor

A mentor is not necessarily someone who provides you with money. He supplies you with something much more valuable than that: time.

People often equate a mentor with a means of making money—someone who sets you up, hands over a lump sum like an angel investor, and checks in with you once in a while to make sure you haven't gambled it all away. Not so fast. Have you ever made $10? Have you ever spent $10? I take it you said yes to both. Okay, now: Have you ever made $100 and spent it? I'll assume yes again. Clearly you've made money and you've spent money. You usually can get back your money, but you can't get back your *time*. How many of you can get that same ten minutes that you had ten minutes ago?

A mentor can help with money, but first and foremost a mentor is appreciated for his or her time. I've thanked all the mentors I've had along the way for sharing their mistakes, lessons, directions, tips, advice, words of caution, and words of invaluable wisdom. These things often don't necessarily relate to money. They get downloaded into you through the gift of time.

How do you find a mentor? Even if you have many wonderful, supportive friends and family members, I recommend finding a third-party mentor who knows a lot about the specific field you've chosen to enter. (And if you don't know yet what field you should be in, hang tight. We'll be getting to that soon.) Find out who's already in your industry and doing well. Ask around, get some names. Then call them on the phone and flat-out say who you are and what you want. Don't assume they will automatically know you want them to be your mentor. No one reads minds. Specifically say, "I've heard great things about you and admire you. I've been trying to learn more about and get into [name field/industry] and would love for you to be my mentor."

Once you get past the fear of picking up the phone and taking the initiative, you'll find magic in conversation. Many of us fear the rejection of a cold call or cold e-mail. But you have to make that initial connection. Magic can happen after you get up the nerve to take that first step, but it won't happen spontaneously while you're just sitting there. I receive letters all the time from people asking for mentorship or who want me to hire them at one of my companies. Occasionally I do invite some of those people to come work for me, and I do mentor a few individuals who catch me when I'm available to read and respond to their intriguing letters. If it's any consolation, even celebrities and people of influence have to make cold calls and pitch themselves over and over again. That's partly how they remain on top; they can't continue to be on everyone's radar by relying on media hits alone.

Asking for a mentor is good practice for building other skills, like obtaining clients and marketing a business venture. When you're trying to build a reputation and promote yourself, you don't target just one person. You target as many as possible. Remember, be everywhere all the time, letting people know you exist. When my first book came out, I didn't sit and wait for *Essence* to call and congratulate me on my bestseller. Among the many marketing tools I employed, I immediately sent out 30,000 e-mails to get speaking engagements and schedule promotional events. The law of averages says that with 30,000 e-mails out there, it's more probable that I'll get a response than if I send zero e-mails. Wouldn't you agree?

> Always look at your life as the Law of Averages. The more frequently you put yourself out there, the greater chance you have at getting what you want.

Don't be afraid to ask "so-and-so" to be your mentor. You never know when you're going to reach a given person with your letter, and she just might say yes.

Years ago, when I was fifteen years old and sitting on the Board of the Las Vegas Chamber of Commerce, I introduced myself to Wayne Huizenga, owner of the Miami Dolphins, just before he was about to speak. I simply said, "Hello, sir. I wrote you a letter." He responded, "Yes, Farrah Gray . . . how are you? I loved your letter."

I was ecstatic that he'd actually read my letter. Stunned, actually. The lesson: Don't underestimate the power of letters (especially written ones). But e-mails can work, too. And don't shy away from inviting more than one mentor into your life. I've had many along the way and will continue to reach out to others. The law of averages operates in this regard, too. Contact more than one person when seeking a mentor. Continue to seek out other mentors as needed. You will be evolving over time, and fresh mentors with innovative insights will help take you to new, higher levels. The more successful you become, the more mentors you will need. Of course, you can also become a mentor to someone else, which is a beautiful way to give back. It completes a cycle in life.

When people tell me, "I want to be rich like you," I reply, "No, I want you to be *richer*."

Get Uncomfortable

If you are in a job you hate, I bet you are "comfortable" but unhappy. It pays just enough for you to survive and you count the minutes of every day, wistfully looking toward the weekend or your next day off. Getting uncomfortable can be any number of things, from finding a new job or trying a different field, to starting a business and being your own boss. No one can stay comfortable and happy forever. The things we find in the zone of discomfort should be welcomed as tests of life, and without them, life would be a boring sea of sameness. There would be safety there, but there would be little to no point in living. That kind of life is reserved for people who rely heavily on good luck and who fail to plan or work. Those types usually don't get very far. When you seek out discomfort, which is what this book is teaching you to do, you can then embrace its inherent power of forcing change and adaptation—two secrets for people to prosper and enjoy a rich, fulfilling life.

Play with a Winning Attitude

Lastly, a little note about attitude that speaks for itself: According to studies done at Harvard and Stanford University, when a person gets a job, 85 percent of the time it's based on the person's attitude, and 15 percent of the time a job is secured, it's based on the person's skills. This shouldn't be all that surprising. How many times have you run into people who are so negative that you don't want to be around them? Well, if you don't want to be around them, imagine how other people feel—people like potential employers, potential supervisors, potential mentors, potential business associates, potential clients, and so on. How many opportunities are lost because of poor attitude?

Once you realize that the world is more receptive to people with a positive attitude, your best bet is to develop your own. How to you do this? Two tips:

- When you consider your life and your opportunities, think, "It's possible!"
- Surround yourself with positive people. Chuck D from Public Enemy probably said it best: "If I can't change the people around me, I change the people around me."

THE BASES ARE LOADED, GET READY TO HIT

This book wouldn't be complete without sharing inspiration and ideas for starting your own business. I am, after all, an entrepreneur myself, and I owe a lot of my success to starting ventures. Perhaps the current job market is motivating you to consider self-employment. Or maybe your job is standing in the way of you realizing your maximum growth and potential. You're right to think self-employment can be more meaningful, more pleasurable, and potentially more financially rewarding than working for someone else. All of us are granted an open invitation to ourselves. To reject the offer is to violate the very essence of the human spirit. And it's never been easier to be an entrepreneur than it is today.

The term "new economy" has been used to describe the business climate we live in now, which naturally supports entrepreneurship. Media headlines have characterized "New Economy" superstar stories as "From the Basement to Billions," "Garage Million Dollar Startups," "Mommy Millionaire Inventors," "SOHO (Small Office Home Office) Successes," "From the Hood to Wall Street" and "From Welfare to Millionaire," to give a few examples.

The door is open wide for exploration by the "newly self-employed." The words *self-employed* and *entrepreneurship* are used interchangeably. You can be both your own boss and employee of your company. Yet in addition to the increase in start-ups, the corporate climate has also been experiencing a shakedown, as more and more people encounter forced early retirement, redundancy, or unemployment. This can make the thought of starting your own company all the more attractive. You can make use of the broad range of skills you've acquired over the years and apply them to your own business, or seek out a particular need in society that you can remedy with a special set of innate skills that you have or that haven't been fully tapped yet. You may not even need to think as far as the whole of society; your own local community or neighborhood may be desperately in need of a service you can fulfill.

While self-employment and entrepreneurship may not be the route for all of us, everyone should have the opportunity to experience the independence that working for oneself can provide. You'd be surprised at how many ways you can skin the proverbial cat in the world of self-employment. But I'll also give you hints on how to be your own boss and enjoy all the benefits of being self-employed while working in a traditional setting, if working for yourself and technically being self-employed is not for you. You still can find ways to make your own decisions, manage your own time, and enjoy the rewards of your own efforts.

Coming to know ourselves and stepping out on our own—putting ourselves on the line, so to speak—requires tremendous amounts of inner strength. Which is why in this first chapter I want to drive home the importance of building your self-confidence and self-esteem every day. In Chapter 6 I'll explain

---

REALITY CHECK: When I said it's never been easier to start a business than it is today, I didn't mean it's *easy*. Yes, it's easier than it was twenty years ago, when you had to get lost in library stacks to gather information instead of logging online from home; but there's no such thing as a successful entrepreneur who doesn't experience periods of struggle and seemingly endless moments of self-doubt.

the core characteristics every successful individual must possess.

We can be hard-pressed to acknowledge the wealth of inner resources and strengths we have that can be used to start a business, especially if we're unhappy about ourselves and suffering from low self-esteem. We essentially get in our own way of success, constantly caught in the conflict between our desires and our compromises. In this condition it is indeed difficult to look into the mirror and see that we're worth giving ourselves a little respect. But it is at this very point in our lives that we most need this sense of value and the self-affirmations that can only come from within.

Working for yourself is considerably more demanding than working for someone else. You are accountable for every decision made. In a small business you have to be prepared to do it all, because having a broad base of knowledge across a wide range of skill areas is crucial. I don't expect every reader of this book to be self-employed in a month, in a year, or in ten. But I do think that the fundamentals that successful entrepreneurs know and practice should be learned and utilized by everyone no matter what. These nuggets of wisdom are helpful for moving forward in any life pursuit. Here are a few, many of which will come to make better sense as you read on:

- Show interest in others and value all of your relationships, both personal and professional.
- Take the initiative. It's the driving force behind the passion and fire of your ideas.

- Be resourceful. Resourcefulness taps the creative powers of the mind, helping to achieve personal and professional goals.
- Maintain a high level of energy to feed the passions and efforts needed to promote yourself and your ideas.
- Persevere through difficult and demanding times. Don't avoid what's hard.
- Act determined and have the willpower to stay on the right track.
- Carry yourself with confidence but not arrogance. This will prompt innovation (your big idea) and help you navigate the necessary risk taking.
- Have foresight so you can make adjustments to your strategies and actions as you learn. Keep pace with changing markets and changing times to know when to fill the gap and create something new. (We'll see this concept again when we talk about adaptation in a later chapter.)
- Be willing to take calculated risks so you can continue to move forward and capitalize on new opportunities.
- Think profit. Imagine a limitless income and celebration of your achievements. This will motivate you to venture forth on your own and endure the struggle that comes with the territory of business ownership: "no pain, no gain."

In this chapter I've given you a lot of ideas and starting points to contribute to your foundation. You're not ready to bat yet, but when you do step up to the plate, I hope that you astonish yourself. Remember, few things happen on the first try. Even great baseball players only get a hit every three times at bat.

> The empires of the future are the empires of the mind.
>
> —WINSTON CHURCHILL

2

The Work-Hard Lie

Lie: I have to work hard and be willing to make sacrifices to be rich.

Truth: Work less, make more. Find your area of excellence.

A few years ago I had a seventy-five-year-old man call me with terrible things to say, cursing and testing my willingness to listen. He was mad and frustrated that I had been successful and he couldn't understand why I was rich and he was poor. This man had been watching me on TV and wanted an answer to explain his misfortune. I asked him, "What has God put you on this Earth to do?" He quickly said, "I'm a singer." So then I asked him to sing for me, which he did. It wasn't what you'd call a Grammy-winning pitch.

"Sorry, but you're not a singer," I said to him. "Go figure out what you should be doing. Ask yourself three questions." I gave the man a simple exercise to do, the same exercise my goddaughter had done and that you'll be doing in this chapter. I ended by saying, "Then come back to me once you've tried." I also said to him that once he completed the exercise with honesty, and used it to change his life, he would find himself working much less and making much more. In short, he'd be *rich*.

WORK LESS, MAKE MORE

The idea of working less and making more money sounds impracticable and idealistic, doesn't it? Society teaches that if you work hard and do the right thing, eventually your ship will come in. So how did a kid who grew up in Chicago's most notorious projects end up with a net worth of millions? Simple. My success is not an accident; it is always the result of high intention, sincere effort, direction, and skillful execution. It wasn't mysticism or magic; and, as I just explained, it wasn't luck. I created a plan and put that plan into motion. I work hard today, but not in the same sense you might be thinking.

Growing up poor, I used to wonder if God had picked favorites and if so, what had we done to get such a bum deal? We were good people. We prayed all the time, especially my grandma. She was the kind of woman who read her well-worn, taped-up Bible as she listened to the late great gospel singer Mahalia Jackson sing "God Knows the Reason Why" and "I Don't Know About Tomorrow" repeatedly through the day. Grandma used to say that hard work always paid off. Mom said the same.

These sentiments only confused me more because I'd never seen anyone—man or woman—work as hard as Mom. So I couldn't understand why we had to struggle so much when it appeared that we were doing all the right things to be "rewarded with success." What about all of that "a hard day's work" rhetoric? When was it going to be "our moment in time"? When were the big paychecks going to kick in? These were the questions I had at eight years old.

Our dire financial situation made me even more curious about the habits of people who had money. It was hard to imagine, but I knew that there were people in the world who never looked at price tags. There were people who ate at nice restaurants three or four times a week. People who took lavish trips around the world. People who drove expensive sports cars and lived in humongous mansions on rolling hills. I figured they must have all the answers.

By the time I hit the ripe old age of nine I'd begun to take daily trips to the library to devour self-improvement and business books and titles by and about successful people like they were going out of style. I listened to all of the authors give their take on success. Many of them said the same thing: If you're a good person, then you can become rich and successful. But I soon discovered that was a steaming pile of crap. Being a good person, while certainly one of my core values, doesn't necessarily have anything to do with achievement. If it did, how do you explain how insanely rich people continue to make headlines for doing some not-so-good things? What explains good but poor people? How does working hard lead no nowhere but the same old hard work?

Now I was even more perplexed.

So I dug deeper and asked myself, "Can money really make

your life perfect?" No, it can't. In fact, you can have all of the trappings of success—real estate, cars, and 401(k)s—but still may be quite damaged on the inside. I now know one universal truth: Anyone can make it to the top, but if the ladder's leaning on the wrong wall they'll likely end up in an unfortunate situation.

The older I got, the more I learned that happiness wasn't a by-product of financial prowess. Integrity and caring for others are far more important than the size of your bank account. Money is just transportation. You see, money may not make the world go 'round, but it does make it easier to travel to the places you want to go, literally and figuratively. That's why I prefer the term reallionaire to millionaire. Because I know that if I become the wealthiest man alive but have no character and no conviction, then I'm morally, emotionally, and spiritually bankrupt, and that's an avenue I trust I'll never have to walk down.

The idea of working less and making more is based on this truth: Once you find your area of excellence, things will come together in a way that makes work relatively easy and fun, and the results you achieve will facilitate becoming rich beyond your wildest dreams. What's more difficult—being successful and enjoying it or being unsuccessful and miserable, wondering what's wrong with you? The work-hard lie is just another excuse to avoid putting effort and focus into your passion. The truth sitting right beside this lie is that it's only hard work if you don't like it! Moreover, working hard is not about devoting more hours to your current job or pretending to be happy at it. It's feeling inspired to go after what you really want, so much so that any sacrifices or dues become welcome growing pains.

THE WORK-HARD TRUTH

Work less, make more.
How do you do this? You find your area
of excellence.

Millions of people have worked for many years but have not been able to materialize the things they wanted. Why? Because in all likelihood, they haven't stopped to explore their area of excellence. When you're doing what you love to do, there will be some days when you don't have to do much work at all, or you don't even notice that you are, in fact, "working." It's not that you won't have crazy busy days, or moments when you're stressed out and tired to the max, but the good days will outweigh the frustrating days. You won't complain so much about work, because it will be something you enjoy no matter what life decides to throw at you. Opportunities will abound, and you may even find checks coming in from places you never thought possible. (I'll explain the beauty of this later.)

Unfortunately, you can't take work to the bank. You can't make a cash deposit of time, effort, and energy into a bank account. Likewise, you can't get good credit terms by showing how hard you work. As I said in the previous chapter, the universe is impersonal. Banks don't appreciate the process or what it takes for you to make a deposit; they only want the product— your money and evidence that you know how to handle it if they are to offer you good credit terms. Work alone is not nec-

> REALITY CHECK: You can work, work, work, work, work, but if you're not working in your area of excellence, if you haven't asked yourself the three upcoming questions, then you're working aimlessly.

essarily a currency for success, but a combination of skills, passion, drive, hustle, and ambition does make for valuable currency. You have to take your talents and what you do best, see them as potential paths to success, and then work toward making them successful.

Here's another way to look at it. If you're going thousands of miles in the wrong direction, think how much farther you are from where you want to be. In the meantime, you've used up precious energy, time, and effort. It's like the exchange Alice and the Cheshire Cat had in Wonderland when she asks the Cat which direction she should take. He says it depends on where she wants to go. And when she replies, "I don't care where," the Cat quickly says it shouldn't matter then. But as Alice adds that she'd like to go *somewhere*, the Cat assures her that she is sure to do that . . . if only she walks long enough.

I find that most people talk vaguely about what they want to be in the future and where they want to go, but the key is making plans to get there. Do you want to just go "somewhere," or do you want to go to a specific destination? If you have a real goal in mind, then you must make real plans. If you are walking through the forest and have no real plan, you could end up walking in circles all day and end up lost. Life is like a forest. You have to make real plans to get to a real destination, and that destination can't be a hazy, blurred target. When I say real, I mean it.

Plans aside, you can't start making them without a potential destination. You do have to start *somewhere*. And that means making an initial goal of pinpointing your life's purpose. I see the truth in that old quote that the richest place in the world is a cemetery. It's where unfulfilled dreams lay dead, where people are six feet under with talents and gifts they never used, embraced, appreciated, and shared with the world. They never painted the Picasso or Jacob Lawrence picture that was within them; they never wrote the book that could have changed literature; they never played with their passion in cooking to become the next Barbara R. Smith or chef Emeril Lagasse. I recently was struck by a man who came up to me after a speaking engagement to express how deeply sorry he was that he hadn't known about these three questions sooner. He said, "If someone would have given me those questions years ago, I would be in a different place today. I'm pissed. The questions make it so easy. I wish I had known."

THE THREE QUESTIONS

Let's get right to those questions. They will help you take inventory of your skills and interests, starting with what you know as opposed to what you *don't* know.

> The two most important times in a person's life are:
> when we are born, and when we know WHY we were born.

1. What comes easy to you but harder to others?

Think about what people compliment you about. Certainly you have at least one or two things that you do well, and which get other people to notice. The reason others notice and offer a compliment is usually because it's something they aren't that good at themselves. They even may say that you're weird because you have this special, unusual talent. People are admiring your natural skills that they lack. It doesn't have to be a profound skill; it can be based on an everyday or common activity like writing (poetic) e-mails, cooking (amazing) meals, or creating (beautiful) flower arrangements.

Sit down and really think about this question. Write down what comes to mind. What do people say you are good at? What natural abilities do you have that you may be able to make a living with? Keep in mind that most everything we do is simple to us. Many times our powers are so great that we are unaware of them, which is why they get ignored. You probably take more than half of your hidden talents for granted. *HELLO!* Let's see if we can't yank them out and capture them as bona fide opportunities.

2. What would you do nonstop even if you never got paid for it?

Think about things you absolutely love to do regardless of the money. Everybody knows someone who hates his job but loves to get a check. That moment of receiving the money, however, is fleeting. Imagine having a great time making money from whatever you're doing, but the money is just a bonus. The money is not the reason for what it is you've chosen to do. Most successful people I speak with don't talk much about the money part. What they do share is how easy it is to get lost in their work because they love it so much. If you can fall in love with your work, then the money will take care of itself. So I ask you again, financial security aside, what could you consider doing for years without ever getting paid to do it? Create a new list and write down what you come up with. Put your passions before any concerns about money. Think about what activities or areas of interest truly capture your spirit and get you excited.

3. How can you be of service and give back to others?

The more we give, the more we receive. I believe strongly in that. At the end of the day, to know we made someone else's life better is very satisfying. The third question to ask yourself is how you can give back to your community and the world at large. This is a very personal piece to the equation, and it's far-reaching. Giving back can entail anything from volunteering, donating, teaching what you're good at, and supporting local charities to providing a much-needed product or service that you know people want. Sometimes time is the way to donate.

Giving doesn't necessarily refer only to nonprofit or service-oriented jobs. You can be adding value to society just by filling a need or enriching it with your talents through a product for sale, advice, or making other people's jobs easier. As you grow, you likely will need employees or temporary workers, so to that extent you're providing jobs and giving opportunities to others. At some point your giving for profit can turn into giving for the sake of just giving. Bill Gates created Microsoft to bring the power of computers to the world so people like you and me could benefit, but look at what he's doing now with his success. He's a champion donor and founder or supporter of numerous charitable organizations and foundations that span the globe and affect the lives of billions. The fruits of his labor at Microsoft, from the day he decided to investigate how to make a computer a household item, are now nourishing the world at large on a massive scale through innovation in health and learning.

We never want to be selfish. Another reason to ask yourself this question is to get you thinking less selfishly. That one slight shift in your thinking can help usher in more ideas.

OKAY, NOW WHAT?

I've never had anyone come back empty-handed after doing this exercise. When you start asking these questions, certain things automatically stand out. They probably are the things that you like to do and that come easy to you. Oprah loves doing her show because it comes easy to her. Gladys Knight's voice flows out like it's nobody's business. Tiger Woods hits golf balls effortlessly. His playing is natural to him. That's who he is. If you were to try to sing like Gladys, you might not sound quite the same. If you were to watch Tiger and then go try to hit like him, you might not strike the ball with the same finesse. Whatever you come up with using these questions is what you need to start paying attention to. You will find out if you're truly meant to be a doctor, lawyer, accountant, writer, scientist, singer, artist, teacher, project manager, software developer, and so on. You will begin to explore ways of turning your natural capabilities into businesses or higher versions of your current self.

When Trish M. asked herself these questions, she instantly identified interior decorating as the place she needed to be. She loves the field of design and finds herself offering tips on furniture arrangement and decorating everywhere she goes. Friends and family members routinely compliment her style and ask for help in decorating their homes and offices. Her eye for color, fashion, and spatial layouts is unmatched by anyone she knows. The third question didn't faze her a bit; she wants to offer a high-end service for profit but also build a nonprofit component to her business to address underserved areas in her community. She'll choose a few families a year and go in and help them vamp up their homes, which has the added benefit of contributing to the beautification of entire communities. At the time of this writing, Trish is still mapping out her plans and building up her reputation as a freelance decorator while she continues her current job as a bank teller. She's been a bank teller for eight years now and is ready to make the shift. I commend her efforts and look forward to watching her future blossom.

SKILLS VERSUS DESIRES

One of the biggest contributing factors to failure is the failure to discern between a skill and a desire. A desire is a general interest in something. "I like astronomy." "I like basketball." It's not too smart to say that you want to be an astronaut, though, if science and math are your weakest areas. Likewise, it's not a good idea to say you want to be a professional basketball player if you didn't make the high school team year after year. However, if you are good at a musical instrument, perhaps a career in music may make sense.

Desires tend to make for lofty, unrealistic, and vague goals: *I want to be a millionaire. I want to go to the moon. I want to be a movie star and ride around in limos. I want to play in the Super Bowl. I want to sit in the front row at the Grammy Awards.* We all have our own version of these types of desires, but they typically are not tied to any specific skills and are so broad and sweeping as to be downright ridiculous. See if you can get more explicit with your desires based on *your* skills. You will be using them as your launchpad rather than the reverse. Trish didn't say she wanted to be an interior designer (her desire) without acknowledging a skill set already in place to match that desire (her eye and recognized talent for design and decorating).

When people ask me whether it's okay to learn an entirely new skill because they think they will be good at it, I say it's far easier to consider what skills you know you have rather than to explore new ones—especially at the start. You can always learn new skills, but there's typically a reason why you possess a particular set of skills already.

REALITY CHECK: Your skills are the *things that you are capable of doing*. They reflect more than a general interest or fascination.

Look at the subjects you were good at in school or outside in life. Are those things solid enough to build a life around? Are those things strong enough to turn into a career? You have to take inventory of the things *you are capable of doing* in order to define your actual skills. Once you define your skills, you can begin to set your goal for success and create a new vision for yourself.

GOALS VERSUS VISION

Immediate goals often relieve you of an undesirable situation, such as getting out of debt or clearing up your credit. They also can be positive steps you take in your blueprint for success. Your long-term vision, on the other hand, propels you toward great possibilities, like owning your own business or being a highly respected professional in a particular industry. A vision encapsulates your goals but goes much further than honoring the little steps you take each day. Your vision also must take in your morals and ideals; they must resonate with your values if you are to enjoy the journey. If you are not excited about what you're doing with your life, you probably won't get maximum results. This is a clear indication that you are not living your life's purpose.

You have within you everything that you need to achieve your goals while fulfilling that vision. One goal at the start here is to learn how you work. How can you put your values, beliefs, assets, liabilities, strengths, and weakness to work for you? Your assets and liabilities are one and the same . . . depending on how you approach them.

In life we are either driven by promise or pain—the promise of an abundant future or the immediate need to change a painful situation. Whichever is motivating you, set the vision. Then do the work. This will move you in the right direction. Monitor your progress every week and every month. If it helps, make a chart. Don't change the goal, even if you fall behind. And if the process goes in a different direction, do not be afraid to change the course and follow it. We'll revisit this recommendation again. It's important to be able to recognize when something isn't working and find a solution. This means being prepared to make many negotiations along the way.

State what you envision for yourself, and try to attach a realistic timeline:

My Immediate Vision: _____

    Completion Date (Goal): _____

My Short-term Vision: _____

    Completion Date (Goal): _____

My Mid-range Vision: _____

    Completion Date (Goal): _____

My Long-term Vision: _____

    Completion Date (Goal): _____

Now, ask yourself the following:

- Do these goals match up with your skills, talents, and what you want to accomplish? Are they realistic and practical?
- Can you measure these goals? See if you can break them down further with mini-goals and apply them to a calendar. Aim to track and measure your progress.

NEGOTIATE WHAT YOU WANT

Negotiating what you want entails two things: 1) the weight of risks and 2) the potential benefits. Both of these encompass the first part of what I call "doing the knowledge."

Life is a series of negotiations, starting within yourself and then extending out to include others. It's smart to be honest about the potential risks involved in a pursuit and weigh the pros and cons of everything—at every step. If there are more cons than pros, then you probably don't want to try that one right away. Keep your strengths and weaknesses in mind, too. Analyze them on paper. Compare them with the skills necessary to do well in a particular pursuit. We tend to know when we shouldn't start off in a particular area. I wasn't the best student in a school setting, so I knew that being formally schooled to be, say, a surgeon, just wasn't for me. If adding, subtracting, and multiplying don't come easy to you, then being an accountant probably isn't in your DNA. For many people, an inventory of skills and desires will result in a number of choices attuned to your unique DNA.

You may have an aptitude for a particular area of study but also a strong desire and interest in another area of study. At that point, the benefits of each choice must be weighed, and whichever offers the most potential is probably the best choice.

Being able to distinguish the difference between a risk too high to take and one that could launch your success is a very personal endeavor. I implore you to use the Z-to-A approach: Start with the end in mind. People tend to get caught up in the excitement of the beginning and forget to think about the end. Be realistic about what it will take to reach that end point. Think in terms of time, money, and the ability to sustain yourself in the meantime. While it's true that many people break through at the last minute—getting their big break the day after they've decided to give it one more day—you need to be comfortable with the risks you decide to take.

It's also true that many successful people have bet on their stability—their homes, cars, and tangible assets—for the sake of money to get a business going. But this is risky and could cause more problems than you ever intended, affecting your relationships with family and friends. The safest risks are those that bet on time and effort more than money and financial stability. As you entertain risks that put your livelihood on the line, you really have to listen hard to your gut instinct to see if you can find a more cautious approach. Let the strength of your aptitudes help guide you in the decision-making process. Be real about those aptitudes.

MAKE TIME, DON'T LOOK FOR IT

There's another big lie hidden in the time factor. It's the "I'm too busy" lie, which I don't think makes much sense. The universe is still impersonal on this one: Everyone has the same twenty-four hours a day and seven days a week. Time doesn't play favorites. Successful people don't have more time than other people. But they do know how to make time by way of how they prioritize and manage those same twenty-four hours, 365 days a year.

Let's admit it, we always find time for the things we want. If you don't make time, you don't want to do it. Stop trying to look for time to magically turn up for you to go pursue a dream. Time won't stop just so you can catch up with yourself. If you think you should be doing something but are having difficulty making the time, then find someone who can help inspire you and be a source of accountability. Tell that person, "Hey, I need to spend at least three hours a week making plans toward X, and I want you to check in with me to see that I'm living up to that."

Drawing a clock on a piece of paper can help. Slice it like a pie. Count the hours and minutes you already are committed to on an average day, with work, kids, chores, etc., and see where you can devote pockets of time doing some of the things you want to do. Thinking and believing we don't have time is a disease. *I don't have time to go to the gym. I don't have time to work on this project. I don't have time to think about another job.*

There's a certain level of denial in the busy lie. It may be human nature to get caught up in "busy-ness," but it shouldn't be natural to let busy-ness consume you. We let our lives go by without listening to ourselves. How can we come to understand what we want and make plans to get there if we don't listen to ourselves?

Nothing should be more important in your overall schedule than having YOU time—be it for building on an impassioned skill set or taking a restful time out to regain your strengths and spirit (which then helps fuel the engines for playing with your passions). I have a few secret places I escape to for deep self-reflection and meditation. These are my self-proclaimed sanctuaries where I can shut out the noise of the world and ignore all the little stuff that gets in the way of seeing the bigger picture. I emerge feeling replenished, acutely in tune with myself, and a more effective individual. This ultimately allows me to be a better person on all fronts, from a personal and business perspective. The safety precautions on an airplane say it best: "Put your oxygen mask on and THEN secure the child or person next to you." This is the Law of Preservation. You have to take care of you first, and nurture your own survival tactics. You must schedule time to do things for yourself first. Because if you don't, who will? Who says he's too busy to get rich?

The Busy Lie: I'm too busy to do anything else.
The Busy Truth: Busy-ness is an excuse. Never say that you're too busy. People make time for the things they want. Driving a thousand miles in the wrong direction will keep you busy, but then what? Ask yourself: Are you too busy to get rich?

"I'M TOO OLD"

You're never too old or young to do what you're intended to do. This was made outstandingly clear to me in 2006 when I had the opportunity to spend time with chaplains at various hospitals. My sister had been undergoing treatments for leukemia, and I often found myself asking questions that relate to the experience at the end of one's life. I thought I might learn something that would help me live a richer, more fulfilling life.

It's common knowledge that people in their dying days have regrets. But not regrets about what they did. On the contrary, they regret what they *didn't* do. They speak of opportunities that they didn't pursue or attempt. They regret never taking advantage of a certain prospect. They wish they could leap back into time and into a healthy body again to take that chance or dare.

Besides, what's the standard that says you're too old or young? Remember, I don't know who "they" are. You probably don't, either.

Although the saying "live life to the fullest" has become a cliché, we must remind ourselves of just that every day. When you self-reflect, which I recommend doing every night, ask yourself: Am I happy with who I am? Am I happy with who I am becoming? Your answers will help guide you in your decision-making the very next day.

Watch out: You are likely to encounter the age lie—that you're either too old or too young—numerous times in your life. First you'll be too young, then you'll be too old. And no one will appreciate you when you're somewhere in the middle. Why not? Because the timeline doesn't exist. It's an arbitrary piece of senseless noise from society. People have been telling me for years "When you turn eighteen it's over . . . when you turn twenty it's over." I get the other complaints as well: "You're too young to be so rich. You're too young to be so successful." Then there are the people who tell me that I'm "done." Every few years, I hear people say I'm "toast." *Thank you for sharing* is what I say in my mind.

Tune out society's clatter. It will never go away, so it's up to you to ignore it. In the next chapter we'll see the importance of reinventing yourself, which gives the people who spew the age lies an endless run for their money.

DO THE KNOWLEDGE AND GET AHEAD

Education and training are important; they are the second component of "doing the knowledge." You need to have a root knowledge, not a branch knowledge, which means you can't just skim the surface of a subject and suddenly become the master of it. Having comprehensive knowledge requires digging deep, even if you are ahead of the game with a bundle of natural skills for a particular subject at the start. You can never have too much knowledge, but you can have too little. And a little knowledge usually is dangerous. That's when you're likely to take too many uncalculated risks and enter a minefield ill-equipped.

Once you have defined your goals and vision, you have to figure out what it takes to get there. Study your chosen profession. You can acquire that knowledge in school or in life. This is where mentors and teachers come into play, people who can give you the information you need to move forward, especially at the starting line. They often make for great cheerleaders, too.

Even the cream of the crop have coaches, teachers, and mentors. Famous singers have singing coaches. Olympic athletes have coaches. Actors have acting teachers. Bestselling authors have editors. Dancers have choreographers. Directors have producers. Professionals like lawyers, doctors, and scientists have mentors—those senior to them who know more through more experience and can inspire new ways of thinking and problem solving. We all need someone to help us take our raw talent and transform it into polished talent. We also need people who can challenge our thinking and get us to see a different perspective from time to time.

Trouble is, as witnesses to (and for some, envious admirers of) other people's success, we typically see the end result rather than a progression of practice, practice, practice. When we watch a star perform onstage or a runner dashing to the finish line at the Olympics, we forget to consider all that went into that single winning moment. We skip over the hours upon hours of missed attempts and fine-tunings that helped usher out that now dazzling performance of talent. We are in awe of the *outcome* but fail to acknowledge and appreciate all the *in-come* leading up to it.

I'm a great example. No one sees me reading, researching, studying, or practicing my speaking skills in front of the foggy bathroom mirror in the morning. It may *look* like standing before an audience is something I can do on the spot, no preparation necessary, but let me be the first to tell you that I continually work on my speaking skills. I seek ways of improving upon my skills as an orator, writer, and businessman every day. It's naive to think that innate skills can get better and better all on their own. Every singer has a sound check before any performance. So will you before you go out and do whatever it is you're intended to do.

> Do what comes natural to you, but then go
> get the training for it.

For those who need more structure and a process to handling decision making, let me share with you my AHEAD methodology. It can help you track your options mentally and stay in tune with yourself:

A: **Assess** risks from an educated standpoint. Do the research necessary to learn about all the potential risks involved in a pursuit. Don't overlook any of them.

H: **Hear** what enters your mind. Don't underestimate the power of gut instinct when weighing pros and cons and taking an honest look at the risks.

E: **Evaluate** thoughts and potential solutions to problems. You'll likely be problem solving from the day you ask yourself those critical three questions. Take your time thinking through what you need to do in order to move forward. Think through every step and direction you decide to take. Consider other options along the way. Be open to circumstances that change your surroundings.

A: **Act** based on experience and self-examination. Make calculated moves. Like the game of chess, see if you can act with your third move in mind.

D: **Discern** between what's working and what's not working to continue forward. This is when you might need to plan a new direction. We all hit walls once in a while. That doesn't mean we have to stop. We turn around and find another way. We have to be willing to let go of the ideas and pursuits that clearly aren't working. They should be placed in the desire category instead of the known-skills category. For example, if you thought you could be a football player but you've blown out your knees and can't rely on them as you could in the past, maybe it's time to switch gears and admit that this pursuit may not be working. You've hit a wall, but there's an open road to be taken elsewhere with another set of your innate skills.

You can employ the AHEAD method pretty much anytime. It can be used for small-scale decisions, such as what to wear on a job interview or where to enroll in a class that will help you master a skill set. It also can be used for those larger, life-changing decisions, like where you choose to live, work, and start a family.

PAY ATTENTION TO CATALYSTS

For a reaction in chemistry to happen, you need certain ingredients. Take water, for instance. Most of us know that water is made up of two hydrogens and one oxygen molecule, hence H^2O. You can't have water without these ingredients. No oxygen, no water. No hydrogen atoms, no water. I want you to view success in this manner as well. You need to have certain ingredients to support a reaction that will result in your success. If you don't have enough of a particular ingredient, you won't have the outcome you're seeking.

So what kind of ingredients am I referring to here? The same ones we've been talking about and will continue to talk about: drive, ambition, hustle, confidence, knowledge, plans, and a clear destination. Just as water won't magically form out of thin air, success won't, either. If you are low in supply when it comes to any of these qualities, work toward replenishing them or nurturing their abundance. Start with affirmations, explore my three questions with a realistic inventory and evaluation of desires versus skills, and pay attention to catalysts.

Another aspect of chemistry that can help you to see the overall picture is having a catalyst. Catalysts accelerate the rate of a reaction—they get reactions going. If you've ever tried to light a fire by rubbing dry sticks together, you know that's a slow way to go. But introduce a match with phosphorus (a catalyst) and you've got a fire in no time. Catalysts are there every day in the real world, but we tend to ignore them until we are ready to acknowledge their existence and then do something as a result. Catalysts help keep you focused, charged, and full of optimism.

A catalyst can be any number of things, from a business idea to getting inspired by a seminar or teacher, to more serious experiences like losing a job, becoming a parent, or even having a near-death experience.

A huge catalyst in my life was the heart attack my mom had when she was forty-six years young. At the time I was eleven and already in an entrepreneurial mode. But her health scare really hit me and my family. It was a wake-up call to action; I could see a tendency for all of us to become workaholics if we weren't careful. I vowed to take care of my body first, and then everything and everyone else . . . just like those safety precautions on airplanes. It's not about being selfish—it's about being smart, and *able* to take care of all else.

But what troubles me is when catalysts are there and no one notices. Bad stuff happens and people still don't act. Even crackheads won't change until they want to. I call it couch potato mentality: You sit around waiting for something to happen while you continue to live with the same old habits and behaviors. There's no sense of urgency. I can't just tell you to go live on the edge, because you have to find what will motivate you to move. The key is to get inspired, and you can start to do that by asking those three questions. They are powerful and effective and have worked like magic for some people. Think of your answers as catalysts to pay attention to. Also think of the personal decisions you make as catalysts. Then begin to notice other catalysts in your life that get you fired up. They can be small and insignificant or large and life-changing. You never know what they could be. Things are happening to you all the time, but when are you going to wake up? You have to want to change. You can be addicted to self-help books, tapes, and seminars but still go in circles and wind up in the same place. You could be Zig Ziglar's, Jack Canfield's, and even my biggest fan and still never execute the changes to achieve what you really want.

So yes, what you currently are reading must be turned into action. Which is why I want you to put at least one thing into action at the close of every chapter. For this chapter, consider those three questions. Find a way to begin applying your answers to your life today.

THE ARTIST

That seventy-five-year-old man I mentioned at the beginning of the chapter clearly wasn't a singer. I told him that once he was able to answer those three questions for himself, the world and the marketplace would open up to his gifts and talents.

I later learned that this man finally took me—and my questions—seriously. He became a painter, selling one of his works for $5,000. So he knew he was an artist, just not the singing kind. I regret that it took him more than seventy years to figure out that his talents were best served with a paintbrush and canvas. But like I said, you're never too old. This man can now live out the rest of his life a whole lot richer.

Everyone's life has a purpose, and it's up to us to discover what that purpose is. It is the reason for our very existence, and it is our destiny. You can say that you will be the next so-and-so, but if that is not your destiny, the universe will not open up to make that path available to you. It is important to pay attention to your true destiny, because you may believe that you are failing for other reasons, when the failure is simply destiny telling you that you are on the wrong path! Destiny is not something you create; it is something that you *discover*. Once you discover your purpose, your destiny, you have to align yourself with it or you could end up on a path of self-destruction.

The more aligned we are with our sense of purpose, the more we feel a sense of belonging to the larger reality of our mission on this planet. When we are in touch with our purpose, we invite inspiration, power, and value to our lives.

Some people mistakenly look for their purpose from other people. How many times have you heard people talk about finding the person who can give their life purpose? People who talk about family, friends, and jobs that give them purpose, instead of discovering their real destiny in life and taking their purpose from that. Your destiny cannot be given to you by anyone else. It's in the same place it has always been—within you!

BE THE NEXT YOU

A friend of mine once announced, "I'm going to get away from everybody." To that I said, "No, you have to work on you. You're the one person you can't get away from. No matter where you go, you are still you."

"Yeah, but at least I can get away from these particular people bringing me down."

"And why are you attracting them?"

He didn't have an answer. We attract the people who wind up around us, so if my friend wasn't attracting the right kind of people, I believe the problem resided within him—not in the people. If he were to move away, he'd still attract the same type of people but in a different place. What I encouraged him to do was work on himself, because if he's not happy with who he is, he has to change something.

REALITY CHECK: It's virtually impossible to change other people. The one person you do have control over in terms of change is YOU. Remember, great men and women don't always start out great.

Part of the goal of this chapter is to get you thinking in a more entrepreneurial way. The idea of building a personal economy around a job is naive and obsolete, especially when you believe that the job will provide a permanent means of earning a living. This type of misunderstanding can lead to personal and economic collapse.

I meet many individuals at events around the country who classify themselves as "unskilled" or "semiskilled" because their jobs require limited technical skills, yet those same individuals make renovations on their homes, repair their cars, service appliances for friends, and mend toys for their children. These skills far exceed those required for their respective jobs. In short, it is ridiculous not to utilize the wealth of untapped abilities and vocational interests that you already possess. The best way to explore these "beyond-the-job" skills is to provide opportunities to use them in a self-employment enterprise, where your earning potential is vastly increased.

The sky is the limit for the earning potential of an entrepreneurial endeavor. A person working a job for an hourly wage may quickly increase his earnings through self-employment. No matter how good his salary is, the salary usually isn't open-ended, whereas the potential earnings for a self-employed person are virtually limitless.

Naturally, success in self-employment requires tremendous effort, and we all know that there are risks involved. As an entrepreneur, I appreciate how difficult it is to transition from the workplace to being self-employed. Individuals who are accustomed to working for someone else have learned to take instruction and follow other people's rules and regulations. They are seldom recognized for taking initiative. They may feel comfortable with the benefits they are receiving, such as a retirement plan, health care, and vacation and sick days, and are unsure of how to obtain or incorporate those same benefits on their own. These benefits can be taken care of in the world of self-employment, and most of them take care of themselves. So don't worry about them yet. They might make the journey look too arduous and steep at this juncture. Recall that I said successful people, including business owners and entrepreneurs, are developed over time. They don't have to know or do everything all at once in the first at-bat. A logical first step, especially for the Undecided (ahem, you don't know yet what business you should be in), is to list potential areas of personal background, special training, educational and job experience, and special interests that could be developed into a solid business. Find a business that you like and understand. Pick an industry you already work in.

Also bear in mind that being your own boss doesn't always mean you have to get an MBA or be a noted expert in a given field. You simply have to develop an effective system from concept to creation, research to reality, and idea to implementation. You have to do your homework and engage in self-examination, because being successful requires a realistic understanding of all sides of your personal equation.

Whether or not you become self-employed, you must continually assimilate new concepts and ways of doing things. You will learn a great deal about people and your own abilities as you begin to do your homework and explore. You'll also become more mindful of your strengths and weaknesses, which will help you (continually) take an honest look at yourself.

As I have indicated, many people possess a wide range of skills developed outside of the workplace. People who perform simple job tasks (such a drilling three holes in Plexiglas) can be found at home on weekends rebuilding automobile engines, refinishing furniture, building lamps, making clothes, and cooking gourmet meals.

Take my own story as a case in point: I tinkered in the kitchen with flavors and developed the ingredients of a real moneymaking business for producing and procuring over a million dollars in contracts selling Farr-Out Foods Strawberry-Vanilla Syrup as a pre-teen. It's your turn to rediscover latent skills and reactive old interests. Believe it or not, you have all you need to put yourself to work. If you are seriously seeking employment in the current

---

May I Help You?

The fastest-growing sector in the economy of late has been the services industry. When you take inventory of your skills and personal interests, think about the needs of those who don't have the time or who are unable to do the things that need, well, *doing*. Single-parent families, dual-career families, senior citizens, other businesses locally and globally, and a wide range of diverse consumers all are potential consumers. You can create a new service or offer a variety to one that's already existing. Just as you are willing to pay to get help, so are other people. They also need products, so don't ignore potential ideas in the products industry if your skills and hobbies translate to a new or redesigned product. If you are minimally resourceful and creative, you can identify a niche in the marketplace.

economy, why not consider hiring yourself? Why not be the next YOU?

Once the decision is made, it's only a matter of working out the details.

IMAGINING LIFE'S COMING ATTRACTION

Each moment can change the rest of your life and the course of your direction. If you are not intentional with your actions, you will plan to fail. Successful people operate from the beat of their own drum, but they are intentional. Successful people don't become successful by accident—it's sheer practical application. You have to make at least one move toward your goal every single day. You have to dedicate a part of every day to doing what you love. Don't just talk about it. Talk is cheap. You may not know exactly where you want to be or what you want to become. That's okay. You are guaranteed to get closer to your dreams if you just walk forward and begin to question.

Let's return to the concept of work once more. Work is doing what's necessary to get to where you want to be. Doing what needs to be done. Work hard so you can play hard. When you keep trying to do something and it just doesn't fit—problem after problem—then you're doing something wrong. You can't do anything unless you put work into it, but working in the wrong direction will always leave you unsatisfied and unfulfilled. You are likely to be broke both financially and spiritually when you've traveled thousands of miles in the wrong direction.

Try to recognize any resistance when things are not falling into place over and over again. This is a sign that you should go back to the drawing board and ask yourself, What am I doing? People sometimes try to fit a round peg into a square hole. When you are walking the true path, things come together and you notice a difference. You still will have classic bad days (I like to say those are the days you get paid for!), but they don't hold you back in the long run. Those days may feel like stumbling blocks, but you're still headed in the right direction.

Albert Einstein once said, "Your imagination is your preview of life's coming attraction." That phrase encapsulates so much of how I live each day. Remember, when you think positively about your future, leaving the past behind, you can attract what you want. And it's your imagination and no one else's. I challenge you to take what I've already given you thus far and start to imagine your future. Imagine your own coming attraction, and watch those planning ideas arise.

What would you attempt to do if you knew you could not fail?

— ANONYMOUS

3

The Celebrity Lie

Lie: I have to hit it big in the entertainment or sports world to be rich.

Truth: A celebrity is someone who is celebrated— someone who shows up to do something well.

Ask a group of people why they aren't rich and chances are many will say something like, "Well, I'm not a movie star and I'm not in the NBA." Do only celebrities make money? Why is wealth so strongly associated with celebrity-dom? Because our culture—with its ubiquitous fascination for the glossy entertainment and pro sports worlds—perpetuates this fallacy on a *daily* basis. One doesn't have to go far to be hypnotized by this lie; celebrity news magazines, the media in general, and even *Monday Night Football* keep it alive. The truth is that the bank accounts of celebrities pale in comparison with the richest people in the world. And I wouldn't call celebrities rich who are unhappy, unsatisfied, and constant tabloid gossip as a result of unscrupulous acts.

CELEBRITIES ARE THE CELEBRATED

The number-one reason most people don't get what they want is that they don't know *what* they want. At the same time, they *don't know what they're passionate about.* So they haven't a clue what they are supposed to be doing. Hopefully by now the lessons of Chapter 2 have given you a starting point. But now it's time to really conquer the lie that runs too deep in our consciousness and takes us off the course from the road we should be taking.

Pop quiz: Who is Ingvar Kamprad? Who is Ursula Burns? Who was John H. Johnson?

Answers: Ingvar Kamprad is the founder of IKEA and the fourth-richest person in the world, with a net worth of $28 billion. He turned a love for peddling matches, fish, pens, Christmas cards, and other items by bicycle as a teenager into an empire selling furniture and household goods to the world at large.

At this writing, Ursula Burns is ranked as the 27th Most Powerful Woman on *Fortune*'s renowned list. As president of Xerox Corporation, she helps bring in billions of dollars a year in revenues for the company and is one of the most respected businesswomen in the United States. As a member of the Xerox team for more than twenty years, she calls the company her family and she wouldn't still be there if she didn't love what she does.

The late John H. Johnson was born in Arkansas in 1918, the

grandson of slaves. He went on to found the Johnson Publishing Company, an international media and cosmetics empire, head-quartered in Chicago, and became one of the richest men in the United States. Today his empire includes *Ebony* and *Jet* magazines, Fashion Fair Cosmetics, and EBONY Fashion Fair. Johnson was the first black person to appear on the *Forbes* 400 Rich List, and had a fortune estimated at close to $500 million when he passed away in 2005.

I'll give you one more example: Janice Bryant Howroyd, the founder of Act-1 Group Staffing and Professional Services. She went out on a limb when she started the company in 1978 from a single office in California, and now it's a multimillion-dollar business spanning the country with a network of more than seventy offices. In 2003 *Black Enterprise* magazine named the company the third-largest African-American owned business in the United States. In 2006 it boasted $718 million in sales revenues.

What do these four individuals have in common? They are celebrities in their own right. They are highly respected and admired. They set the bar for many others in their industries and communities at large. But they aren't routine newsmakers in the entertainment reports; the paparazzi don't follow them and they don't always get to walk a red carpet. In other words, they aren't celebrities in the usual sense of the word. They are men and women who are *celebrated* for what they have done—what they have shown up to accomplish.

THE CELEBRITY TRUTH

A celebrity is someone who is *celebrated*—someone who shows up to do something well, which may have no relation to the entertainment or sports world.

WHAT TO DO WHEN YOU'RE
NOT THE NEXT IDOL

For those who aren't entertainers or athletes and don't have the chance to draw from the rewards that those stations in life bring, there are other options. The possibility of success exists whenever we are able to define our area of excellence and flourish accordingly.

I get frustrated when people tell me they dream of being a celebrity in the usual definition of that word. It's a selfish endeavor to try to be a star. We often idolize other people without knowing if they are good with math or kind to their mother. We also don't recognize and acknowledge all the work and practice that goes into being a celebrity. Not all celebrities are selfish. True sports stars like Tiger Woods and Hollywood starlets like Beyoncé and Jennifer Hudson are doing what they are meant to do. They have found their purpose, and it just so happens to be one that puts them in the public spotlight.

But I know plenty of people who are much richer than most celebrities. I also have heard lots of stories (and so have you) about people who made it big as celebrities and then lost it big. Some get their fifteen minutes of fame, whereas others last a bit longer. Consider all the celebrities who have filed for bankruptcy. Wayne Newton, the iconic Las Vegas entertainer, filed for bankruptcy in 1992 with more than $20 million in debt. He's paying it off through his contract with Stardust Hotel, which reportedly is paying him over $25 million a year for performing forty weeks a year for ten years. Stanley Burrell, also known as the musician and entertainer MC Hammer, filed for bankruptcy in 1996 because his lavish lifestyle exceeded his income and his pockets were empty when lawsuits arrived on his doorstep. Bankruptcy aside, others have been known to lose themselves to psychological problems, breakdowns, or dodgy acts that evict them from the limelight.

I would not be where I am today had I pursued becoming a celebrity. That would not have utilized my talents and gifts. It's dangerous to believe the celebrity lie, which often goes hand in hand with its familiar cousin—the lucky lie. Celebrities frequently are viewed as lucky people who wake up one morning to riches and red carpets. That's just not true. They are ordinary people who become extraordinary by virtue of their willingness to pursue their talents and show up.

We see the costs of believing the celebrity lie every day on shows like *American Idol*, especially in this day and age when becoming a celebrity and getting rich looks as easy as appearing on a reality show. But we witness people doing things they shouldn't be doing on those same reality shows. Some of us may get intoxicated by watching other people's dreams, but be careful. In the true reality show of life, we should be focusing on what *we* want to do, and what *we* are good at.

You see, there's no limit to your wealth and popularity if you are doing what you are supposed to be doing. The tag "celebrity" offers people respect and recognition. Well, you can have that in *any* field. You can be a famed physicist, a popular engineer, a respected doctor, an admired store owner in a small neighborhood, a trusted and highly sought-after community member who organizes events and speaks at local gatherings. We all would love to receive awards, but for some reason we focus on the awards that make headlines, like the Pulitzer and Nobel prizes, or have to do with television shows or movies, like the Golden Globes and Oscars. While those are great goals to have if they are aligned with what you should be doing, be aware that there are more awards out there than you can imagine. You certainly can find one to honor your accomplishments regardless of the field you choose. Remember, Ursula Burns is ranked as one of the most powerful women in the United States on *Fortune*'s list, John Johnson landed on the *Fortune* 400 Rich List, and Janice Bryant Howroyd was twice named by the Star Group as one of the 50

REALITY CHECK: It is human nature to crave recognition and rewards. You will be noted in your field if you put in the time and effort. Don't get caught up in wanting to be a celebrity. I can't reiterate this enough: Celebrity means someone who has been celebrated. That's it. If you focus on your own gifts and talents, you, too, will be celebrated.

Leading Woman Entrepreneurs of the World. Who wouldn't want *that* kind of acknowledgment?

PASSION FIRST, HONOR AND RESPECT SECOND

In interviewing a woman for a secretarial job, I asked her where she saw herself in the future. She said, "Oh, I see myself sitting in the front row of the Academy Awards waiting to get my golden statue!" I held my urge to laugh.

"Have you take any acting classes?" I asked. She answered no. "Have you ever been in a play?" She answered no. This woman had no experience whatsoever in acting (so presumably she didn't know whether or not she'd be good at it), and had done nothing to look into the acting field. Yet she saw herself winning an Oscar. She merely wanted to be famous.

People often want to be famous without knowing what famous means. I am recognized every other day; it's a regular occurrence, which might have you thinking I'm famous. I don't see it that way. I have become a TV personality for being successful in my field—starting companies and motivating entrepreneurs. I've gotten endorsement deals for causes such as bone-marrow donation and homelessness. I've been invited to share my words of wisdom on shows like *20/20*, Donny Deutsch's *The Big Idea*, and *Good Morning America*. You may think my time on television and in the spotlight make me famous, but my so-called celebrity-dom was not a result of being on television—it came from my personal achievements as a man of business first and marketing myself and my ideas second. In other words, I earned the honor and respect I enjoy today from the public and from media outlets *after* I already had pursued my passions and found my calling. If you are looking for respect and acclaim from others, you must get it from yourself first and then cultivate that success through your passions. You can't have it the other way around.

Donald Trump became a television personality *after* he had become successful in business. Politicians become personalities *after* their success, which is what won them the votes. Ralph Lauren became a household name *after* he'd dabbled in fashion and tried to launch a line of clothing. People don't get famous in an instant from an outside source. Lightning doesn't strike them. They earn their fame and glory over time. They build and practice skill sets that shepherd in more and more opportunities. That fame and glory isn't always fit for television, but nonetheless it offers a rich, fulfilling life.

START NEW CONVERSATIONS

Often what separates those who look like they are winning for fifteen minutes, like the hare in the familiar tortoise vs. hare race, and those who can endure the long run and come out the real winner in the end (like Mr. Tortoise did), is the ability to "start new conversations." No matter what field you choose to be in, you must learn to adapt routinely and reinvent yourself from time to time. Again, my story is a prime example. I started by painting rocks that I found in my neighborhood and selling them door to door. Did I know then that eventually I'd sell whole businesses to the tune of millions? Or own a magazine? Or be a motivational speaker, author, and syndicated columnist? Of course not! But the little successes I had in my daily journeys continued to generate fresh opportunities for the taking. Clearly I could not have planned all these opportunities, but I was ready for them when they arose. One plan led to the next. Each new opportunity allowed me to refuel and reinvent myself. That's how I had checks coming in from places I had never thought possible back when I was selling rocks, mixing syrups in the kitchen, and supporting a local group of young urban entrepreneurs. I would not be where I am today if I didn't reinvent myself over and over.

> **REALITY CHECK:** Finding an area of excellence is just the beginning. It's a single defining moment—a starting point—from which to flourish through multiple adaptations and new conversations.

Another example of looking at the bigger picture is the rapper 50 Cent (aka Curtis Jackson). Here's a man who thinks more like a businessman than a celebrity, and who got a whole lot of new conversations started. When Curtis Jackson first received an advance in the music industry, he didn't rush out to spend it all on trinkets and toys. That would not have gotten many new conversations started, or if it had they would not have lasted long. Instead, he invested in buying a trademark to his stage name, 50 Cent. That name is now worth millions. And don't be too quick to think that all comes from his singing and acting career. Indeed, he qualifies as a bona fide rap star now, but the decisions he made from his initial launch led to a sustainable fortune unheard of in the music industry.

While many may not agree with what "50" (as many call him) often represents in his music and videos, we all can appreciate the struggle he faced as a young man. To go from the violence and strife of the South Jamaica section of Queens, New York (and his well-publicized history of drug dealing and having survived being shot nine times), to owning licensing and endorsement contracts, plus shares in a company, took grit, focus, and determination. He truly lives up to the title of his popular semiautobiographical film: *Get Rich or Die Tryin'*.

As a youth, 50 Cent represented legions of urban youth who saw their circumstances as their all-encompassing reality and realm of possibility. The urban environment is an island in and of itself. There are walls all around this island with mirrors on the inside. People living there typically are growing up to understand that they only can be what they can see. 50 Cent managed to see beyond the island and break through those self-destructive mirrors. He also was able to look beyond the lottery mentality that hangs around the music industry and hip-hop culture in general. This ultimately allowed him to spot and capture new business ideas; the endorsement deals and licensing agreements that he has secured over the last couple of years arguably are doing more for him than his musical talent. He's been reinventing himself since that very day the music world honored him with a check, delving into ventures such as fashion, footwear, entertainment, record labels, ringtones, videos, and even water with vitamins. These ventures amassed revenues of about $50 million in one year. But wait, here's the kicker: Of all the ventures in his pocket, the one that has produced the most returns has been a growing energy drink company. As a 10 percent shareholder in Glacéau, a Queens-based manufacturer of bottled water infused with vitamins, he received about $400 million from a single deal. In 2007 Coca-Cola offered the company $4.1 billion in a buyout, just three years after 50 Cent agreed to endorse Glacéau's new grape-flavored line of vitamin water, Formula 50 (50 in honor of 50 Cent, but also because it contains 50 percent of the Food and Drug Administration's daily recommended vitamins).

Who knew a rapper and water would be such a lucrative mix? I doubt 50 Cent just takes the money and spends it wildly. He can now continue to reinvent himself and reinvest in new ventures that beget more deals. Opportunities and new conversations abound.

> There is no excuse for a one-hit wonder. When you have a hit, that's the time to work even harder. That's when you work ten times harder to create multiple streams of income and reinvent yourself time and time again.

Stella B. is another person who started a new conversation with herself, albeit regrettably at first, and far from the realm of celebrity-dom. Growing up in a middle-class family in Los Angeles, she was surrounded by an aura of celebrity but didn't want to become one. Early on she had her sights set on being a doctor.

From the age of about five Stella naturally gravitated toward science, and biology in particular, and it seemed like a perfect fit—at least all the way through her high school days. She always dreamed of the day she'd don a white coat and tend to sick people. She wanted to make a difference in the world and witness the improvements made in medicine afforded by new technologies and research findings. Medicine had been in her family, so it felt good to live up to a few legacies. In her gut it felt like a calling, and she felt that having a medical degree would bestow upon her a certain level of respect and admiration. For Stella, being a reputable doctor was like being a celebrity in her own right. It also helped that she loved formal education and her parents could afford to send her to good schools.

But the tides turned when she started college. That's when things got rough. Even though she already had groomed herself to be a doctor for years by this point, she struggled through college-level science and math. The plans she had made more than a decade earlier simply were not working out. Keeping her head up high and maintaining her persistence, Stella forged onward and did what she could to stay above water. She played by all the "rules" that were invisibly written for pre-med students: work in a research lab, get published in a scientific paper, volunteer at local hospitals, learn a second language, be diverse in your studies but mostly focus on the courses that will help you survive the medical boards, and so on. She pulled an untold number of all-nighters throughout her four years of studying chemistry, calculus, and physics—the three subjects that gave her the most trouble. She thought she was in decent shape after performing well on the medical boards at the end of her junior year. The dreams of wearing a white coat were now in plain view. Or so she thought.

Doomsday hit within weeks of graduation the following year, when not a single acceptance letter arrived in the mail from the multitude of medical schools she had applied to. Everyone said no. Rejection across the board was hard to swallow. All her life she'd been the good student who did everything just about "right," but now when she was supposed to cash in on all that good work, a wall came up. With feelings of utter defeat, Stella didn't know what to do. Persistence wasn't paying off. The conversation she'd been having with herself for the majority of her life now had to end.

This type of rejection can be difficult to overcome. It can cast a person into a sea of self-pity and a sense of worthlessness. Time to reevaluate and reinvent. Stella had to figure out what she'd now do after graduation. She had no job lined up, and she didn't know where to begin looking. Whether it was part of her DNA or just part of her training, Stella went into survival mode— doing the very things I'm teaching you. She took inventory of her skills and interests, trying to figure out how she could transfer all that she'd learned as a pre-med student to another career. She could have landed a job in medical research, but being a lab tech was not something that got her excited. Clearly life was telling her that she wouldn't be a doctor, at least not at this time. She could apply again in a few years, but for now she had to do something else. The rejection was more than a sign; it was a catalyst for change.

It didn't take long for Stella to have an aha moment. She'd

been studying science and math for so many years that she could count them in her box of skills even if she didn't apply them in the medical world. Those skills gave her a unique ability to think critically, analyze, and problem-solve. She could take something complicated like the anatomy of the human heart and break it down into parts that she could understand and memorize. She could perform computations relatively quickly and turn technical language into everyday words. This is when, through her soul-searching, Stella discovered another skill: writing. While she was passionate about biology in college, she'd also nurtured a love and knack for reading and writing. If she wasn't attending science classes, she was immersed in literature courses. Professors had complimented her on her writing, and some even said she'd be an author someday, which she figured meant she'd publish medical studies. Never did she think that what her professors said would predict the path she'd eventually take.

That is, until those rejections came piling in. Now what? Looking back, Stella saw only one thing she could do, and do well with gusto. While some of her friends attended medical school in the fall, she enrolled in a writing class at a local university's extension program. She moved back home and focused solely on writing. For the first time, she was thrilled to get up early and stay up late. It took but one month to realize that writing was her true calling. To make a long story short, Stella fashioned herself into an established science and business writer, and never looked back at medicine.

When Stella reflects on the years she spent toiling with lab reports and Bunsen burners, she calls them her training days. They endowed her with a way of thinking that few other writers get under their belts. "I wouldn't be able to do what I do today had I not taken all that science and math. I employ those skills every day, and it's come in really handy when I have to write an article on a technical subject, or help a doctor bring a complex idea and topic down to earth for the everyday reader. I wouldn't trade this job for the world. I'm independent and totally self-sufficient."

Within ten years Stella went from a drowning pre-med student to working as an editor in a small publishing firm, to finally owning her own writing and editing company. She loves learning new things every day, broadening her skills as she tackles new subjects—just as a doctor would do when diagnosing a patient. When I slipped one day and uttered the words *hard work* to her, it was she who corrected me.

"Hard work? What 'hard' work? Trying to be a doctor was 'hard work.' What I do now is *not* work! It's my life, and I love it."

GET REAL WITH PLANS

All the people I've described so far didn't have to figure out the gritty details to their plans at the very start. When 50 Cent started rapping in a friend's basement, where he used turntables to record over instrumentals, he probably wasn't thinking about contracts with water companies and Coca-Cola. His area of excellence prior to that was in drug dealing and getting into trouble with the law. No sooner did he shift gears and dedicate his mind to *legal* deals and writing music did he tap an honest and true passion . . . and find a path to riches beyond any drug dealer's dreams. Stella B. could not have known she'd be an established writer back when she trudged through pre-med courses miserable and stressed out.

If you can visualize your goals, even if they are just a few short-term ones at the start, then there's a strong probability that you can achieve them. Good plans don't have to be a hundred pages long with endless detail, but every plan should start out with a basic list of aims and a reasonable idea about how to accomplish those aims. The most important thing to remember is that plans are not set in stone. You can change them at any time based on experiences that you learn along the way.

With an idea or two in mind from the exercises you did in Chapter 2, plus a realistic understanding of your skill set and knowledge, the next three things to consider are how to:

1. Size up the goal and start planning
2. Have a Plan B
3. Focus on the positive and be ready to adapt

Size Up the Goal

Many times our goals seem insurmountable. But if you worry too much about the long road ahead and forget to enjoy the journey, you can get caught up in the anxiety and succumb to exhaustion. When this happens, try to break it down and look at smaller portions of the goal. For example, if your ultimate goal is to become the head of your own record company, it would be practical to think about the process from step one to the finish line. You should think about finding artists, then finding other people to work with you, such as publicists, managers, promoters, and so on. Then you have to think about getting the records made and where you will go for distribution.

And if you don't have a goal, try this: Make it your goal to get a goal! Just don't make "success" the goal. That's too vague. To say you want to be successful is a given, but it's not the hope of a great achievement or a plan to accomplish a specific goal. Rather, success is an *attitude* that affirms the worthiness of who you are and the things you are doing. It is an attitude that keeps you open to new discovery and continual growth. And you can't really work toward success without specific goals.

> You can make it a goal to get a goal, but don't make "success" the goal. Success is not a goal. It's an *attitude* that affirms who you are and what you're doing. It's also an attitude that keeps you open to discovering more about yourself and your continued development.

Once you have a goal, you can break it down into smaller steps and then create a plan of attack. Are you a butcher, baker, or a candlestick maker? Your ideas at first may not appear to you as big ideas that can go to market. But don't shoot any idea down. If

Howard Schultz hadn't envisioned a world where coffee and coffee stores could be sexy, there would be no Starbucks. A young man living and working near a college campus in Jackson, Mississippi, opened a small chicken-wing restaurant that was met with rapid success. What was so great about his idea? He was selling "the sizzle," not "the steak," with eighteen different sauce flavors to choose from, which kept the college students coming back for more.

Choosing a business idea that will work well is the first step in starting a business. Here are a few questions and ideas to get your creative juices flowing, some of which we'll be revisiting later:

- Could you do your current job working for yourself rather than being employed by someone else?
- Could you turn a hobby into a business?
- Could you copy an idea? An idea does not have to be novel or even original; in fact, very few businesses are based on original ideas. Observe what happens abroad or in another town—you could get an idea that has not been tried where you live. Look around, watch the news, be observant, and think how you could translate what you see into a business idea.
- Look for inspiration: You could be inspired with an idea by looking at trade magazines or attending business expos or trade shows. This could provide the seed for a new idea or give you an idea to do something better. Try brainstorming with friends and family. Invite them to come up with any ideas (it does not matter how silly some of them

may sound). A brainstorming session should last no longer than fifteen minutes. It should be used as a starting point to help you think about the opportunities available.

Apart from choosing an idea based on your skills, you could research markets you believe might be profitable. The ideal market would, for example, be a growing market and have a niche. Get to know and respect the competition. Identify direct competitors (both in terms of geography and product lines) and those who are similar or marginally comparative. Much of this can be done online at first. In fact, you might find too much information on the Web and not know how to sort through it. Be patient, and take your time. Try to apply the results of your own research in the context of the industry as a whole. This will allow you to make more valid projections and be aware of the trends and special industry considerations to help you operate your business effectively. Analyzing the market is how you gather facts about potential customers and determine the demand for your product or service. Industry associations, industry publications, media coverage, information from the financial community, and their own marketing materials and Web sites may be good resources to identify these things and rate the performance and position of each competitor. The more information you gather, the greater your chances of capturing a segment of the market.

After that, put your efforts into generating something that people actually want, take their money in exchange for your product, or service, and make sure your product or service costs less to create than you charge for it so you have enough money to keep the cycle going. Whatever business idea you decide on, also think about how it would work on the Internet. Consider the following:

- Public appeal: Can your idea be marketed to attract customers and appeal to their imagination?
- Transportability: How will you transport your product or service locally and around the world? Remember, the Internet makes it possible to have customers on the other side of the globe.

Whether you've decided to start planning a business or go back to school and switch careers, I recommend that you write out your plans (more on business plans in Chapter 6). You also may want to consider using a calendar to map out goal points. Time spent in planning pays for itself because it will make you more efficient, and the process forces you to take an objective and critical view of the project in its entirety. There are a number of good business-planning books and even software programs to help you

REALITY CHECK: The world is full of talented people, but what makes one person fail while another succeeds? It is the blueprint and goals you establish for yourself that allow you to move from conversation to implementation and on to success.

do this. They can help you understand the various aspects of business operations and how they relate to each other, as well as help you to develop realistic goals and procedures to implement a business plan. A great site to check out is *The Wall Street Journal*'s Startup Journal (www.StartupJournal.com) and CareerJournal (-www.CareerJournal.com).

Have a Plan B

Not everything goes as planned. But you can't just strike out. While you need to have a goal and make plans to move toward that goal, many plans fail because of factors beyond our control. For example, let's say that you plan on playing professional football. If you are a very skilled athlete and are already playing college ball, that's not an unreasonable goal. However, if you get an injury that prevents you from continuing to play, if you also are studying a vocation, that injury won't be the end of the world. Which is why you should always have an alternate plan at hand. It can be smart to put effort into more than one endeavor.

A few years ago I met a man at a banquet who was very accomplished in real estate. I had been looking forward to meeting him because of my own interest in real estate, and it turned out that he, too, had been wanting to meet me in person. We connected immediately and our conversation eventually led to making plans to open a real estate brokerage together. At the time it seemed like a no-brainer. The market was booming, especially in Las Vegas, where homes were doubling and tripling in value in a short time period. The potential to literally get rich quick in real estate was, shall we say, very real, but as we were about to find out, very fleeting. Las Vegas was experiencing a gold rush, and even Californians were flocking there to buy homes on the cheap that were "guaranteed" to be worth a lot more in little time. At one point I learned that four thousand homes were being purchased a month. So I naturally imagined our brokerage house cutting thousands of deals a month and taking our percentage. I was very excited to get a piece of this gold. So was my new business partner.

But most good things do come to an end, especially one *this* good. We planned the brokerage in 2005, and by the time we opened our doors, the Vegas market was crashing faster than a brick from a building. Talk about bad timing. We'd already invested hundreds of thousands of dollars in our new venture, including two offices and people we'd already hired on payroll. These people had left other companies to be with us. As the market spiraled downward, real estate agents fled; more than 26 percent of agents who had just gotten their licenses were leaving the market. Homes went into foreclosure because people were stuck in exotic mortgages—having gotten locked into 100 percent loans with no money down. Some had fallen prey to predatory lending schemes. When their homes devalued, they found themselves underwater and unable to either refinance or sell. Those who tried to sell at a loss had homes sitting on the market for eight or nine months. Experts were saying the climate would only continue to crumble.

My business partner and I had some decisions to make. We hadn't even opened our doors yet and we were losing. Our instincts said to abandon the idea. In fact, I recall that in our first of many meetings one night we planned to call it quits. "Let's close," were our words. We were ready to jump ship and accept the loss. Then, by the next morning we had both changed our minds. "No, let's do this. Let's move forward. Let's figure it out."

We asked each other, Where is the money to be made? At first, we agreed on "nowhere." But then we dug deeper. We started asking questions that might help us ride out the storm and find other ways to make money. We thought about what we could do differently but still make money. We had no revenue, but we had months of overhead, plus people who had committed to us. Since many real estate offices were closing, we had to adapt. And that meant brainstorming on how to create a service that was still needed or that was going to be needed *because of* the fate of the market.

"Why don't we become an REO company?" my partner suggested. REO stands for Real Estate Owned. It was a brilliant idea. We'd essentially become a holding company on behalf of banks for the sale and purchase of foreclosed and pre-foreclosed properties. This meant approaching the banks (the lenders) who were taking properties back from those who couldn't keep up with their mortgage payments. We offered to represent them and facilitate the resale of properties that had been foreclosed, and we would get a percentage of the sale. A*ha*!

This plan B worked. No longer dealing with producing agents and trying to work the cranky, slow, and depressed real estate market on the homeowner/consumer side, our clients now were the big banks that do millions of dollars worth of volume. Because banks technically are not in the business of buying and selling homes, having us to do that for them would be like having a full staff at home to take care of things for you while you go about your business. Let me explain a bit further. When a bank takes a home back, it needs a savvy real estate firm to move the property—one that can maintain the property, get needed repairs done, help the current tenant get out, and then go find a buyer. Because we often sell the home for a deal, I feel like we're selling the American dream.

Today my partner and I have ten bank clients and we hold at least $30 million in listings each month. Yet another example of how I can wake up one morning and have more money in the bank. Overnight, three, four, or five offers would come in on homes in the listing. And I didn't do anything but wake up and greet the day. I'd say it was well worth the investment and the setup to get the REO going. Good thing we didn't turn back; we learned to adapt and found a plan B.

Best of all, because of the relationships we've forged with these banks, which include some of the largest financial institutions in the world, we now have awesome contacts and resources to call upon in the future. We've lengthened our list of connections for potential future projects, expanded our network, and essentially broadened our world of opportunities. And we take nothing for granted. When a bank turns over millions of dollars of inventory to you, you have to be the best that you can be. They don't want to work with anything less. Faith and confidence in yourself becomes paramount.

Focus on the Positive and Be Ready to Adapt

Almost any motivational book worth anything will talk about focusing on the positive rather than the negative. If you can't find any other good reason for trying, take this into consideration: We can only think of so much at once, so why not make it something positive? I've already gone over this, but it bears repeating: When a problem presents itself, we can fret all day long about all the bad things that can happen, or we can focus on what we stand to gain. Once we focus on the positive, it's easier to stay motivated. It's also easier to see how to adapt and make the shifts necessary so you can continue to move forward. The stories in this chapter attest to that. Sun Tzu wrote about these timeless principles in the Chinese military treatise he wrote during the sixth century B.C. Pick up a copy of *The Art of War* sometime. You'll gain a greater appreciation for adaptation and compensation. If you can change your strategy quickly, think on your feet, and be a cold-blooded realist, you'll win. And you *will* be celebrated. I guarantee it.

> A new idea is delicate. It can be killed by a sneer or a yawn; it can be stabbed to death by a joke, or worried to death by a frown on the right person's brow.
>
> — CHARLES BROWER

4

The Money Lie

Lie: I have to have money to make money and be rich.

Truth: The path to millions starts with one dollar.

With so many people sinking in consumer debt, maxing out credit cards, and living paycheck to paycheck, it's no wonder this lie remains alive and well. Psychologically speaking, if you are deeply in debt, chances are you'll have a hard time getting past your worries about money to ever picture yourself flying around on a private jet, lounging in your palatial backyard, or having a platinum credit card that you can pay off every month. Keeping up with bills and bosses can make anyone myopic and unable to envision a richer life further down the road. In fact, you can't even *see* the road past where you are currently standing—at the bottom of a pit with no extra money in sight. And the thought of being wealthy while in some debt doesn't make sense, either.

We'll get to the debt lie in the next chapter. Yes, you can have debt and be rich. But first we have to tackle this money lie: If money begets money, then how do you get rich without any? Ready for the truth? Here it is:

THE MONEY TRUTH

It doesn't take the kind of money you think it does. The path to millions starts with the first dollar.

Every success story, whether large or small, can be traced to specific traits, habits, and behaviors. And since successful people do things that render certain results, it makes sense to imitate those actions. These essential actions weren't given to me in a manual when I was six years old. The Great Oz didn't walk into my room one day and say, "Son, here are the rules. Read 'em. Digest 'em. Live 'em" (although I wish someone had!). There were no classes, no audiotapes or seminar series on these powerful lessons—at least not that I'm aware of.

Instead, I discovered these timeless riches over time. What I learned is that the path to success is universal but it's also expansive, so there are many ways to get to the same results. In other words, there are many ways to make spaghetti. If you talk to ten different people, you're likely to get ten different recipes. In the end, though, the dish is still spaghetti. And although each individual may have added his or her own signature style, at a very basic level, spaghetti is spaghetti.

That said, let's be clear about one thing: I said above that success can be large or small. Success can also be short and sweet or long and maintained. Different sets of behaviors and actions translate to whether or not your success will last a swift second or a long lifetime.

For instance, when many people receive sudden financial windfalls, they often return to the same financial state as before and even have been known to declare bankruptcy. Why? Because they haven't changed their behavior toward money and spending so they could hold on to that newly acquired wealth. Evelyn Adams won the New Jersey lottery not just once, but twice (1985, 1986), to the tune of $5.4 million. Today the money is all gone and she lives in a trailer. William "Bud" Post won $16.2 million in the Pennsylvania lottery in 1988 but now lives on his Social Security.

People who are accustomed to having lots of money and then losing it, on the other hand, tend to gain it all back plus more because they think, act, and behave in a certain way that promotes perpetual wealth. While learning the ropes to managing money well takes time and practice, anyone can do it. It's not nuclear physics. A good starting point is getting what money you *do* have under control, including debt and credit. Once you get into the habit of managing money well, you'll never go back to being flat-out broke, no matter how much money you make in the future. And if perchance you do hit a little ditch, which is entirely possible out there in the real world, you'll be able to rely on the same techniques to climb out again. In this chapter I'm going to give you a set of strategies to maximize your income. If you use what you learn here, you'll not only begin to chip away at debt, you'll also soon have those few dollars with which you can pursue whatever you want. I'll also give you some ideas on making more money now and in the future.

Remember, the path to millions starts with the first dollar.

DEBT: A FOUR-LETTER WORD

You know that debt is bad, but you may not understand that not all debt is created equal. There are good forms of debt and bad forms of debt. Some nourish a good credit profile for you, while others whittle away your credit, and, most important, your credibility. The chart on the next page puts debt into perspective.

CHANGE YOUR MIND, CHANGE YOUR INCOME

Getting into healthy habits when it comes to money is step one. Imagine not having to actually think about putting your financial house in order, because knowing what to do to reach your goals comes naturally. Wouldn't life be so much easier (and less stressful) if you didn't have to always focus on making sure you are doing the right thing to support your dreams day in and day out?

I liken this to going on a diet. Diets are for people who haven't trained their minds to automatically think in a certain way that makes healthy living instinctive. The vast majority of

---

Debt: The Good, the Bad, and the Ugly

Debt is like cholesterol: There's a good kind and bad kind. The bad will stick to your financial arteries, build up over time like a nasty plaque, and quite literally cut off any supply of opportunities to you. The good, on the other hand, will help lower the bad, open up those prospecting channels, and boost your overall financial health.

"Bad"	"Good"
High-interest credit cards with balances	Low-interest credit cards, well managed
Forgotten long-term loans (e.g., student loans)	Well-managed loans and mortgages
Debts used to support a lifestyle	Debts used to build assets (leverage)
Unpaid bills, collections	
Consolidated debts that never get paid down	

If you see yourself in the left-hand column—you have lots of debt, no assets, and limited income—make a commitment to shift over to the right-hand side. If you have zero credit, there's only one word to describe that: ugly.

---

those who have achieved optimum health and who maintain their ideal weight year after year don't think all that much about what they eat and how often they need to exercise. Why? Because they practice a lifestyle that supports their health and fitness; they don't need the structure of a diet because they are already programmed to live well.

The mind is a powerful place, which is why we need to start there if we're ever going to see results in the real world. Given the fact that money issues are top on the list of stresses, I'd venture to guess that we spend the greater part of ours days thinking about money from a negative perspective—money is evil, money is too hard to make, money doesn't like me because I can't get enough of it to feel at ease and "accomplished." Sound familiar? Well, let's see if we can't turn that negative thinking around by shifting how you perceive the role of money in your life. We all can agree that money is a means to freedom, education, and comfort. It allows us to grow, achieve autonomy, learn, and provide a value and service to the world at large. Having a positive relationship with money is often the first step to lessening financial stress and making the changes necessary to open new doors to opportunity. To victory. To success.

So how do you change your way of thinking? Start by making positive affirmations about money every day, just as you are doing about yourself. Tell yourself that money is good. Money channels achievement. Money facilitates whatever it is you want to do in life. Don't get me wrong, money is by no means a measure of success, but it's an instrument to help us lead a fulfilling life. And as I've already pointed out, getting what we want starts with the first dollar.

---

*We're all born ignorant, but one must work hard
to remain stupid.*

—BENJAMIN FRANKLIN

LIVE BELOW YOUR MEANS,
BECAUSE IT MEANS YOU
WON'T GO BROKE

If there's one piece of advice we hear more than once but tend to continuously ignore, it's this one. Ignore it no more. Getting a handle on your finances entails a varied collection of mini-steps, some of which may make you slightly uncomfortable at first. If you've gotten used to living above your means, it will be difficult to change your lifestyle and habits. But you must. Start by making small shifts in how you use your money on a daily and monthly basis. Make a journal of all expenses and income for sixty days. Write down everything you spend, from vending machines to car payments. Then, after those sixty days, take a look at your record. You will see where you are wasting money; it's not rocket science. We all have an innate understanding of what's truly necessary and what's not. From there, you can formulate a realistic budget, putting extra money toward credit card bills and savings. You want to be able to meet all of your most critical financial needs while also addressing your debt and establishing a savings cushion.

There are plenty of resources out there to help you tackle your debts and pinpoint where, for instance, you're misallocating your money. Go to my Web site (www.farrahgray.com) for my list of recommendations. In addition to sharing tactical advice on all angles of debt management, including pitfalls like payday-in-advance companies and vicious cycles of late payments, these materials can also guide you through managing which credit cards you should tackle first, second, third, and so on. Cleaning up your credit and confronting your debt go hand in hand. Be patient with yourself; recognizing and amassing your debt (in financial speak, we call debt liabilities) can be an extremely challenging and emotional experience, but it's a necessary step. And no matter how troubled you are by your outstanding balances, you still can find ways to contribute to a savings account and even to a retirement account. The end result is that you'll not only move toward literally being richer, but you'll also *feel* richer in spirit, too. I guarantee it. There's nothing more invigorating than knowing you don't owe someone money for items you've already used up or aren't worth anything anymore.

How much should you be saving? You want to save as much as you can without feeling too deprived, as if you weren't allowed to eat cake or ice cream anymore. It's not an all-or-nothing approach—that would be a setup for failure. But you don't have to spend a whole lot to live well. Sometimes it's not about making more money, but managing the money you have. Expenses always will rise with your income. Studies show that the more people make, the more they spend. Smart savers know that the best things in life really are free—requiring nothing more than an investment of time and love. They also know that the next-best things—the material goods that make life fun—can be purchased wisely and enjoyed for a long time, if not forever. Anybody can change how they're living, no matter where they are. Some people make only $20,000 and don't complain.

I recommend aiming to set aside 10 to 15 percent of your take-home pay. Shoot for 15 percent, but save 10 percent during tight months, and always vow to save 15 percent when you can generate more income. Later, as your income increases, you'll bump up that percentage so you can save even more. At $50,000 a year, you should be saving around 20 percent. And once you start making more money, avoid firing up your spending to meet your new income level. Of course you'll be able to be more flexible with your budget and leverage up your lifestyle, but that extra income is not a green light to spend whenever and wherever you want.

Remember, smart savers—wealth builders—know how to live richly without reaching their thresholds every month. Also keep in mind, especially right now if you are counting your pennies at the end of the month, that each and every dollar counts. You've heard this over and over again, but it bears repeating. Look for 500 ways to save a dollar instead of one way to save $500. Start bringing lunch to work, avoid the coffee houses, limit how much you buy both in retail stores and online (such as music downloads, clothes, electronics), and consider using a debit card that's tied to your checking account so you cannot spend more than what you have available. Bring your energy bills down by turning off unused lights and computers at home. Establish a forty-eight-hour rule whereby you don't buy any unnecessary items (goods or service that are not related to everyday living expenses) that cost more than $50 until you've thought through why you need them now. These types of items can include household goods, electronics, gadgets, clothes, hobby equipment, computer software and games, or whatever you tend to spend money on that is not vital to living. You should be able to pay all of your

Ask Yourself: Do I Need . . . ?

Designer-label clothes: Do online price comparisons for everything you buy! Never pay full price. Buy and sell designer clothes through consignment/thrift stores. Become more concerned with the quality of the fabric versus the name on the label.

Designer phones: Go for a plain vanilla cell phone with basic applications and no fancy features, such as text messaging and access to the Internet, which can be costly. (And even if these features are "built in" to the plan, the plan is probably among the most expensive ones around!) Aim to find a plan that costs less than $50 a month, including taxes.

What 10 to 15 Percent Means:

If you make $30,000 a year, 10 percent is $3,000. If you make $40,000 and save 10 percent, that's $4,000. If you can bump up that savings to 15 percent, you could save $6,000. Either way, that's a lot of money to sock away each year. If you run your own small business and own any real estate, you stand to maximize your tax savings and usher money back to you that can help fuel an eternally running wealth-building machine. Put simply, the more you can save, the faster you can accelerate your wealth accumulation.

Make It Automatic:

Once you figure out how much you can put toward your debt, automate those deductions so they fill up that hole without your having to think about it! Most banks allow for automatic bill paying now. Setting it up is a phone call away. You'll shift your focus from the negative—debt—to the positive—wealth creation. And as you work toward reinventing your life, those debts will disappear, and you can keep your full attention on where you're going—not where you are.

bills, including credit cards, in full every month. If you can't, figure out why; there's got to be a sieve somewhere.

You must create a realistic plan and commit yourself to the things you know you can implement and adhere to in the simplest terms. Change your habits for a reason—not just a season. (For more detailed help on debt reduction, refer to the Resource Guide on my Web site.)

Setting aside all of your collected coins at the end of the day can be helpful. If you were to put all of your pennies, dimes, nickels, and quarters into a jar every day, you'd amass about $20 to $30 by the end of the month. Over the course of a year, that can total $300 or more, which can be put toward your debts or fund a savings account for purchasing future assets.

THE PLEASURES AND PITFALLS OF PLASTIC

How many credit cards do you have? Are they all maxed out? Applying for credit cards in this country has become very convenient with the advent of instant approval, especially when you apply online. You can look into your mailbox and find a bank-issued credit card with your cat's or dog's name on it.

While it's important to keep credit card balances under control, it's also important to learn how to use credit to your advantage. Credit has gotten a bad rap lately because typically it's tied to endless consumer debt. And you may falsely believe you'd be better off with no credit cards. Not so! It's much easier to abuse the privilege of credit than to take advantage of its numerous

> **REALITY CHECK**: Using credit cards should be very much a part of everyone's life. In fact, it'd be nearly impossible to become rich without using credit cards.

blessings, which can help you build wealth and acquire assets.

Credit cards are the number-one way for establishing your *creditworthiness*, which essentially is your reputation for handling debt. If you can't prove that you can manage debt, then you'll have a nearly impossible time getting loans for property, a business, or more credit. You may have trouble landing the job of your dreams. A poor credit profile will also affect which interest rates you quality for, and in some cases your ability to buy solid insurance policies with low premiums. Landlords, potential employers, and auto dealers are all known to take your credit into account when making decisions either in your favor or against it.

If you've never checked out your credit report and score, which is a three-digit number that reflects your creditworthiness, then order your entire report (and score) and start putting your credit profile in order. You can go to a site like www.MyFico.com and learn all you need to know about credit and how it will affect you financially now and in the future. For a completely free report, go to www.AnnualCreditReport.com and view each of the three credit bureaus' profiles on you during any twelve-month period. (Or they can be ordered by phone at 877-322-8288; more details are on my Web site.)

I don't recommend using any credit-repair company that claims it can clean up your credit for you. There's nothing a credit-repair company can do that you can't, and these types of services can be expensive. To that end, I also don't advise that you use credit-monitoring services, either. I want you to start taking responsibility for monitoring your credit profile, which you can do by simply reviewing your report and score at least once a year. Putting the responsibility of assessing your creditworthiness on someone else from time to time is the same as ignoring it entirely. The sooner you tune in to all the goings-on of your financial house, the sooner you will get the results you want. You can't ask your momma to shower, watch your diet, and do the push-ups for you, and you can't do the same when it comes to caring for your credit and debt. Only you can stand at that helm.

How Many Cards Should I Have?

During the process of restructuring your credit card debt, you may be enticed to consolidate down to one or two cards. I don't endorse this approach. While having fewer cards may make you *think* you can better control your debt (including the acquirement of new debt), it's all relative. I'd rather see you expertly manage three or four credit cards than squeeze your financial tools down to one card that you have to rely on for everything. (If you've got upward of eight or nine cards, then by all means try to get it down to four.) Cards with the longest histories never should be thrown out, because they boost your credit score—even if those accounts have not been well maintained. Find out which cards you've had the longest and make sure you keep those. Make it a priority to get those balances under control.

If you're among those who cannot qualify for a credit card because of your history, one of the tricks to the trade is to get two secured credit cards from your local bank, which essentially are cards prepaid via a link to your accounts. Secured cards appear on your credit report in the same way that a lending institution would extend you a credit line. If you can establish a solid reputation for managing your secured cards, soon enough a bank will offer you credit.

Can I Use Credit to Finance My Future?

When people talk about tapping personal funds for purposes of getting a business off the ground, certainly many of those people are talking about credit lines. We hear stories of people maxing out credit cards, taking out second mortgages or lines of credit on their homes, and using whatever credit invitations come their way to help pay for office equipment or even living expenses while writing a novel, screenplay, or doing an internship that doesn't offer any money. There are numerous stories of people

---

REALITY CHECK: You can't always borrow your way out of financial trouble.

who've hit it big by first financing their dreams on credit, risking what could be potentially enormous debt in exchange for a secure future down the line—if everything goes as planned. What we don't often hear about, however, is the story with a bad ending. What's more, a decade of low-interest lending gave us the false impression that we can always borrow our way out of trouble. Fat chance. That "easy money" allowed us to run up debt, but we may be entering a period in which borrowing costs will increase, and new rules to the game entail getting real about what we can handle and planning for worst-case scenarios.

Unfortunately, there are no hard-and-fast rules that I can give you on this. Even though filmmaker and Hollywood business mogul Robert Townsend bankrolled his first movie largely with credit cards some twenty years ago, there are more stories of bad endings to good intentions. You don't want to bite off more than you can swallow, because credit debt can add up quickly and haunt you for a long time (if it hasn't already). If you burn through a line of credit, especially one that's tied to your home and livelihood, and then have no way to start paying it back relatively soon—chipping away at both the principal and the interest—then you're better off delaying the use of that credit line until you've got a steady stream of cash flowing. Cash flow can be more critical to your financial well-being than credit terms!

---

*Think **cash** before **credit**.*
It's easier to increase cash flow than to
decrease credit debt.

Learning the ropes to a new trade or developing your skills in an industry where you know you want to work can be costly. You may have training tools to buy, seminars or conferences to attend, and so on. Be mindful of where you spend your money here, too. I'm not going to tell you what you should or shouldn't do. You have to make decisions for yourself; that's part of you taking responsibility. I'm just here to give you some ideas to help point you in the right direction. Keep action at the forefront of your mind, and don't get bogged down in endless rounds of tutorials that can prevent you from making a move.

MAKE MORE MONEY TODAY

Okay, so you know now that you should be drumming up ways of increasing your cash flow rather than dreaming of tapping as many sources of credit as you can find. Here are three ways you easily can increase your income today:

1. Get a raise
2. Create second streams of income
3. Spring clean (sell on eBay or have a garage sale)

Raising Yourself

Whether you're in a job that has limited upward mobility or you don't think you can ask for more money, there are plenty of opportunities out there for you to investigate. Notice that I've titled this section "Raising Yourself" because it's not about waiting for someone else to give you the handout you've been hoping for. Boosting your income doesn't happen spontaneously. It's acquired *by* you, rather than given *to* you.

● Prepare to have a conversation with your boss about your paycheck. Never think that you can't ask for more money, but do be ready with a game plan. You don't want to merely waltz into your boss's office at nine A.M. Monday morning and say, "Yo, I need [or want] a raise." Think about it: If someone were to walk up to you and start with "I need" or "I want," you naturally would feel put on the defensive. Why? Because those words are all about the other person, whom you are somehow obliged now to please. With that kind of approach, you're not likely to give the person entirely what he's asking for. Neither will your boss. There's a right and wrong way to raise yourself.

For some, confronting the boss about their paycheck is an uncomfortable experience, and avoided at literally all costs. But you need to muster the strength to have this conversation and not wait another year. The secret to doing this successfully is to write out what you want to say first, highlighting specific accomplishments and results in the past that have enhanced *the company*, and what you plan to achieve *for the company* in the future. Have a clear sense of what you want to get, but keep the focus on your boss, his company, and what you can do for him. Don't let the boss decide how much of a raise you should get.

After all, he's not interested in *your* problem; he's only interested in *his* problems, which is why you have to treat the conversation like a sales pitch. You are the seller, and he's the buyer. You're selling your ability to solve more of his problems, and with that comes a higher price. Try to mention exactly what types of problems you think you can solve. Try to find out what your boss needs in order to make his life better, and then try to fill that hole. Be specific. It's okay to make strong promises.

If you haven't a clue how much you should ask for, speak with fellow coworkers about the average raises, but then go higher. Did you know that most employers actually respect those who negotiate better pay? It shows that you're strong-willed, focused, and business-oriented. You're not going to just sit back and accept what's given to you. Instead, you're going to take charge, be assertive, and do what's in your best interests. This kind of attitude translates to the kind of attitude a company needs in its employees. It says you're going to do what's in the best interests of the company so long as the company treats you in its best interest. This is a mutually beneficial relationship.

At a minimum, let your boss know that you're interested in advancing and that you're committed to doing greater things for the company. If you work for a large company, simply making yourself better known to your boss can present new opportunities for you. He or she will remember you and perhaps call on your for bigger projects and future positions that move you higher up.

Tax Tip: Want to see more money in your paycheck without getting a raise or working overtime? If you receive a tax refund each year, then you're probably having too much money taken out of your paycheck for income-tax purposes. You've been letting Uncle Sam borrow your money interest-free throughout the year. You're better off keeping that extra cash and using it to pay down debt and/or save and invest. Changing how much or how little is withheld from your paycheck is easy. You simply complete a new Form W-4 (available at www.irs.gov), and take more personal allowances. Be careful not to take too many or you'll end up with a tax bill come April 15.

● Start investigating new companies or employers who will pay you more money to do the same job you're doing today. Don't settle! Your current workplace may keep you feeling comfortable and at home, but if it's not meeting your bills and you know you can make more money down the road, get moving.

● Work some overtime; just an extra hour a day can add up to a nice annual sum of money. Inquire about special projects that you can participate in and that make that overtime worth the effort. Being a full-fledged entrepreneur may not be for you, but how about an *intrapreneur*—an "inside entrepreneur"? You get the best of both worlds in intrapreneurship, which is acting like an entrepreneur within the safe confines of a company. While still technically an employee of a firm with access to the resources and capabilities of that larger organization to draw upon, you often have more flexibility to do things your way and take on a semi-independent creative role on special projects that are aligned with your unique skills and talents. You follow your company's example but have permission to focus on innovation, transforming a dream or an idea into a profitable venture. Of course, the company reaps the most benefits from your successes here, but they also allow you to become a highly valued member of the organization's team that, for all intents and purposes, feels like the place you are supposed to be. For many people this is an ideal scenario. We saw this with Ursula Burns, who calls Xerox her family and can't imagine being anywhere else. Some intrapreneurs can work from home, while receiving all the benefits that an in-house employee would enjoy, such as health care, retirement accounts, and vacation and sick days. Intrapreneurism works well for people who, for whatever reason, just can't stomach going out on their own and becoming self-employed. With intrapreneurism, you bring the dynamism and energy of life as an entrepreneur to an otherwise static environment. You get to be exceedingly more creative and call the shots but at the same time feel a greater sense of security while in a supportive organization. Intrapreneurism can also be a stepping stone for those not quite ready to leave the nest; it can build their confidence so they are able to become fully independent at some point in the future.

● Increase your rates if you do consulting work, and charge hourly fees. People often feel guilty about raising their rates, but they shouldn't. You get raised by others all the time—at the gas station, by your landlord, the cable company, your insurance company—so why should you still be living like it's 1999? Raise yourself. Your clients won't suddenly pay you more out of the goodness of their hearts.

Create Second Streams of Income

It pays to get creative about ways to make more money. If you've reached your highest earning potential at your current job, then you may want to transfer some of your skills to consulting or freelance work on the side. You can use the talents and skills you are already developing to start a side business and add a second stream of income that boosts your bank account. Soon enough, you may find yourself welcoming more income from the second stream than the first! That's when you know you can safely quit your current job and immerse yourself completely into growing your own business. I've seen it happen time and time again. Recall the story of the seventy-five-year-old artist who finally admitted that he enjoyed painting. No sooner did he set his mind on painting and practicing his God-given talent than he began to see an authentic outcome—accolades and praise for his work, as well as requests for buying pieces at $5,000 a pop.

Got a 401(k) with your employer? If you're starting your business part time while keeping your full-time job, borrowing against your employer's 401(k) retirement plan is a potentially stable investment. It's common for such plans to let you borrow a percentage of your money that doesn't exceed $50,000. The interest rate is usually about 6 percent, with a specified repayment schedule. The downside of borrowing from your 401(k) is that if you lose your job, the loan must be repaid quickly, often within thirty days. This may be an option for when you're truly ready to launch your business, and it can produce an income that can cover any last-minute loan you take from your 401(k).

What I call a third stream of income is taking your talents to a larger event that generates a lot of money. By event I mean a seminar, class, conference, or convention. Even parties or concerts qualify. As a magazine publisher, for example, in the past I've held events that created valuable sources of income—sometimes hitting the jackpot with monies that cover a large portion of my annual expenses in running the magazine. *Essence* magazine does this every year with its mammoth music festival, charging entrance fees from $45 to $110 to see popular entertainers and performers like Beyoncé and Lionel Richie, plus a few speakers like me. P. Diddy started his career as a party promoter—long before his gigs were reserved for A-list stars only.

Because these events typically entail more people, you can make more money. Imagine filling a room with 1,000 people paying $50 each—you can cover your facility cost, promotional cost, and staffing feeds and still have a nice chunk of change left over.

Sell, Sell, Sell!

I don't want to get your hopes up on this one. Even if you get a good tax write-off, you're not likely to make a ton of money through selling your possessions online or at a garage sale (unless you truly find a niche and sell unique items; see page 174 for details on "eBay millionaires"). Let's be real: Used items that over-fill your closets, garages, basements, attics, and storage units aren't ready for the auction block at Sotheby's and probably won't bail you out of debt on *Antiques Roadshow*. You can try, however, turning an old-fashioned garage sale into a consignment shop by enlisting the help of friends and neighbors (who may have Chanel bags and Brioni suits they want to get rid of) and who would jump at the chance to let you do the selling.

The reason I encourage you to do this is because clearing out the clutter, ditching yesteryear's fads, and organizing all that space holds enormous hidden benefits that can support your journey to success. For one, eying all those obsolete gadgets and styles that once cost bundles of money will help you reevaluate how you spend money. You'll feel a psychological lift, energized by having chucked what subconsciously was causing distress and a chink in your mental chain of peace. You may also have the revelation that things don't bring happiness, which will further foster smart spending habits as you move forward and reform your entire way of life. And one of the biggest benefits of all may be finally noticing an empty space that begs to be turned into a profit center. Imagine turning your garage or basement into office space for turning your passions into a river of revenue.

PREPARE TO MAKE
MORE MONEY TOMORROW

Here are the two main ways to maximize your income in the future:

1. Establish *passive* income
2. Get real about your day job, or start your own

Make Money in Your Sleep

Passive income is income that doesn't require your direct involvement. You've already done the work to get the money machine working, and now it operates 24/7 like a well-greased engine emitting more cash for you to collect. Sound too good to be true?

You may be familiar with some kinds of passive income, such as owning rental property, royalties on an invention or creative work, and network marketing. You'll recall the story in Chapter 3 of my real estate company that now allows me to wake up in the morning with a few deals already in the works. It took patience, a few close calls, and some major adaptations to get that venture off the ground and running, but the payoff has been huge. I can't think of a better way to wake up and be excited to get out of bed.

Virtually all wealthy people have some form of passive income. The sooner you start thinking about how you are going to create more passive income, the sooner you can collect more fruits from your labor. While explaining the logistics of establishing passive income is beyond the scope of this book, I want you to become familiar with the types of passive income that you should be considering—if not now, then in the future. (Refer to my Web site for help in finding books and other recommended media to help you prepare for and create passive income.) I'll cover real estate in Chapter 7, but here let's look at two other big categories of passive income that offer a variety of opportunities.

Residual income is a type of passive income you get on an ongoing basis from work done once in the past. Some examples include:

- Business or other consultants who create reports or workbooks that contain their know-how and words of advice on a particular topic or subject area that they can sell online or through direct sales
- Fitness trainers who produce videos or workout and nutrition booklets and sell them online or at the gyms where they teach
- Photographers who makes their photos available through a stock photography clearinghouse and get paid a royalty whenever someone buys one of their images
- Retail owners who have grown to the point of hiring trustworthy managers and can create a product line to market
- Restaurant owners who create cookbooks or brand foods for a product line
- Network marketers and direct-sales reps who make income from their direct customers when they reorder

products every month—classic examples include Avon, Mary Kay, Tupperware Brands, and Herbalife

As you can see, there are many different ways to generate passive income across a variety of businesses. It may be continuous income from the same customers or the sales of a product to new customers. It may require little to no personal involvement from you whatsoever, such as a How-To or guidebook sold on a Web site. Or it may require some personal interaction, such as a sales rep calling customers to remind them about their monthly orders and ask them if they want to make any changes. Distinctions can be made between different types of passive income.

Some types may require more of your involvement to earn the income, e.g., a coach or consultant on a monthly retainer, a real estate agent who shows houses and helps buyers and sellers through the process, or a caterer who delivers lunch every Monday to a local business. While this kind of income can offer welcome stability, it also has its limitations. Your earning capacity will be based on your production capacity, which can be a factor of time and physical realities. (There are only so many hours in the day for you to personally offer a service or lend your hands in producing a product.)

If you can make money from *other* people's work, this is referred to as leveraged income: You leverage their work for your gain. Some examples include:

- Network marketers who build downlines and receive commissions on the sales made by people in their downline

- General contractors who make a profit margin on the work done by subcontractors
- Real estate brokerages who take a percentage of the business generated by their real estate agents affiliated with that brokerage
- Franchisers who license their trademarks and methods of doing business to other entrepreneurs in exchange for a recurring payment and usually a percentage piece of gross sales or gross profits as well as the annual fees. This is the ultimate leveraged income; if you can share your proven way of doing business for money by taking a homemade business concept and franchising it out to other people for copying, you stand to be a giant success. Imagine being the next originator of 7-Eleven, McDonald's, AAMCO Transmissions, Merry Maids, Pizza Hut, Supercuts, or the UPS Store. Every time another person wants to do what you do, you get a piece of their profit.

Intrigued by these ideas? I encourage you to return to those three questions I asked you in Chapter 2 and then consider these:

- Can you create a product/service that people will buy over and over again?
- Can you engage others to sell your product/service?
- How could you make money off the work of others?

Answering these questions will get you started on thinking about how you can find your potential areas of passive income. As soon as you align the responses you got in Chapter 2 with your thoughts on the above, a plan will appear right before your eyes.

Get Real About Your Day Job

Do you like what you're currently doing? Do you see yourself doing this same job five, ten, or even twenty years from now? If you still don't have a clear answer and vision for what you should be doing day in and day out, then you must keep asking yourself questions.

Nothing should stop you from knocking on new doors and risking a step inside, even if you stumble more than once. Lots of successful people have experienced this countless times—so much so that the phrase "extreme failures of the extremely successful" is almost a cliché.

One of the best "failure" stories in American history (detailed in Steve Young's *Great Failures of the Extremely Successful*) is that of Abraham Lincoln's road to the White House: Failed in business in 1831. Defeated for legislature in 1832. Second business failure in 1833. Suffered nervous breakdown in 1836. Defeated for speaker in 1838. Defeated for elector in 1840. Defeated for Congress in 1843. Defeated for Congress in 1848. Defeated for Senate in 1855. Defeated for vice president in 1856. Defeated for Senate in 1858. Elected President of the United States in 1860. **What if Lincoln had given up?**

> **REALITY CHECK:** No one starts out an expert in anything. And no matter what level you place yourself in this world, value the fact that you have the freedom to change where you are.

Babe Ruth spent his childhood in an orphanage and then struck out 1,330 times on his way to 714 home runs and baseball immortality. In 1954 Elvis Presley was fired from the Grand Ole Opry after only one performance and told by the manager, "You ain't goin' nowhere, son. Better get 'all job back drivin' a truck." And the venerable Oprah Winfrey, when fired from her reporting job at the start of her career, was told, "You're not fit for TV."

The lesson (which you'll most certainly hear me say again): You can't win if you don't play. If you don't take the dare, a subject you'll see highlighted in the next chapter, you're just going to sit there. Fortune 500 companies that breed successes year after year have an acute awareness that breakthroughs depend on failure. They explore, experiment, foul up occasionally, and then repeat. They understand that being the best requires innovation, which requires risk-taking, which requires circumventing fear and doing what may feel unnatural at first. When they flop, they spring back up, scrape off whatever insights they can from the experience, and say, "Next!" As an individual, you should be doing the same.

YOUR MONEY IS ALREADY
IN CIRCULATION

Once you get a handle on your debt and credit issues, you'll find money you've never had before—even if your income doesn't change. When people ask me, "Okay, Farrah, now what? I've got a few bucks, but not enough. Where's the money now to get my business going?" I say, "Your money is already in circulation. You just have to access it."

People need to stop saying that they need money to make money. We all can agree that you'd be ahead of the game if you got an angel investor, venture capital, or a small-business loan for your idea. But what if you can't get those things? You have to start out small. It's that simple.

Remember, I started painting rocks. And I made a profit. I started with a dollar and turned it into a million, and then a million more as investment capital became more available to me.

Most people thinking about starting a business fall into one of two categories when it comes to financing their new venture: 1) those who are terrified to borrow money and have a deeply held belief that even if they were willing to attempt getting a loan, few sources of startup capital would be available, and 2) those who think getting money is a piece of cake and there's an endless source of money—most of which is free. Both groups of people are half right.

First, there is no such thing as free money. Many entrepreneurs dream of getting business startup grants. It's important to realize that most government grant programs are really loans, equity investment, or loan guarantees. Keep in mind that even monies that don't require payback in terms of cash do require a significant investment in terms of time and research. Using grants for business financing is a possibility, but you will not get something for nothing.

Contrary to popular belief, most business startups are funded by personal investments on the part of the owner. These people are not wealthy, do not have large sums of money, and are not given any special privileges when it comes to financing their hopes and dreams. These people—like most self-employed business owners—finance their dreams through dedicated work, creativity, and a little help from friends and family. It's much easier to raise cash through your own resources, including savings and people in your personal, inner circle, than to go pitch your business idea to potential investors and strangers who don't know you. Which is why for many people their first deal *is* with family and friends. And guess what: It doesn't take money to make that kind of seed money.

While it's true that some products and services require a bit more money than others to explore, develop, and deploy, especially if you invent something in a particular field, such as communications, you don't necessarily have to start there. Do things in stages rather than attempt to leap to the finish line. If you want to take common items that you have around you and turn them into ideas based on your talent, you don't need a lot of money— you don't need any more money than what you get from your day job. Of course you need money to live, but my point is that you don't need the kind of money that you might imagine. It doesn't require any more money than basic living expenses—eating and having a roof over your head. If you have that kind of money, you can launch something small and build on it.

One of my very first businesses made a whopping $9. After selling rocks I moved on to selling to neighbors body lotion that I had whipped up in my bathroom from unused bottles under the sink. My last customer refused to receive change for her money, and simply told me she was investing in my future. At the time, I had no clue what "investing" meant. All I knew was that I was exactly $999,991 from being a millionaire. Today I have bigger deals coming to me involving much greater numbers, but I don't forget those days of my first sales. I owe all that I enjoy today to those initial dollars and cents that got me going.

> **REALITY CHECK:** It takes money to make money, but don't misunderstand this statement, because the money *is* there. It's waiting for you to access it. Your money is in circulation right now. You just have to go after it.

I read about Markus Frind's amusing story in *The Wall Street Journal* last year. Here's a man who built an online community and *bingo*—became a trailblazer in the Internet dating scene. At this writing he runs one of the busiest, most profitable sites on the Internet, www.PlentyofFish.com, from the comforts of his apartment building in Vancouver, Canada. He is the sole employee of a company that provides a free online dating forum. Who thought that a dating site could be so successful amid the

REALITY CHECK: Start small, think big. For example, you may not be able to launch a magazine, which could require thousands if not hundreds of thousands of dollars, but you can create an online magazine for virtually nothing but time, effort, and the purchase of a domain name. This could allow you to develop a subscriber base cheaply and relatively quickly. Once you develop an online subscriber base, your money is then in circulation. You now have a growing database from which you can sell other products. Even if you have cooked up a grand scheme in your head, it won't cost money to type up a business proposal and show it to other people. If you want to start working on a great invention that no one has seen before; it won't cost anything to share your ideas and spread your message. It can even be something people have seen before; but you have found a way to do it better or reach new customers, which is exactly what Markus Frind did to make his first million.

Match-dot-coms of the world established years ago? Well, Mr. Frind found that there are more dating customers out there than can be captured by any one site, and the fact that he can offer services for free means he can attract lots of, shall we say, fish. So how does he make money? Through Google's small text ads, banner ads, and through affiliate marketing, which other sites pay him for every time he sends them a customer. So if you were to go to PlentyofFish.com, and then link to another site, you'd be funneling money from that new site back to PlentyofFish.com. And that's precisely how Mr. Frind received a $1 million check from Google. The site reportedly brings in between $5 and $10

million a year. For Frind, his money was always in circulation—
out there among the millions of viewers looking for his site.
Looking for a date. Searching for a soul mate. Frind has netted
more than thirsty fish. He's caught boatloads of cash to keep
going and building his business.

> If you drive a Range Rover or a Land Rover and have a land-
> lord, something is wrong.
>
> —ANONYMOUS

5

The Debt Lie

Lie: I have to have zero debt to be rich.

Truth: You must have debt to get rich. You must use debt to get rich.

Not long ago I was having dinner in my office with a friend who reminded me just how bad the debt lie can be. Shanel looked frustrated and depressed. She started complaining about problems we've all heard before: being overtired, overworked, and underpaid. She described how she wakes up at seven in the morning to prepare to be at work by nine o'clock sharp, and doesn't get home until after seven at night. As an insurance agent working for a large company, she's "too low on the totem pole" to gain better control of her schedule. Of her *life*. Money is a big problem; there's never enough. She feels trapped by the demands of the long hours and unable to do the things she really wants to do.

"What *do* you want to do?" I asked her. I thought that was a pretty straightforward question, but she took it to mean small-scale stuff, and talked about not getting to the gym because she's too tired. She's out of shape. Unhappy. Her nails are bitten all the way down. Every day is the same, and she's left feeling unaccomplished, exhausted, and extremely aggravated. It's as if she's being dragged around against her will.

"Why don't you quit your job?" I asked, and waited for her reaction. She gave me that familiar look of *That's a stupid question. C'mon, can't you figure it out?*

"I have a mortgage. Car payments. Bills. I can't just quit my job!" she replied. "I don't want to lose the credit that I worked so hard to build." I knew she wasn't going to like what I had to say, but I had to tell her anyway.

"Let's start with your car. The people who financed you— ahem, the *bank*—are making loads of money off the interest you're paying. Translation: You're allowing *their* children to attend good schools and ensuring they have nice dinners out on the town. Next up, your home. I bet you're paying only interest. You're making the investor—this time, the mortgage company— rich. You're making *them* money."

At this point Shanel was a bit shell-shocked, but I kept her attention. "Don't get me wrong," I went on. "I'm a huge fan of owning real estate. But there are rules to the game. You don't get bonus points for renting from the bank. Let's go to your job. From what I'm hearing you are there for roughly ten hours a day. Guess what I have to say about that. You're making your employer rich. Are you really surprised that you're unhappy?"

"What do you want me to do? If I just stop and quit, I'll be worse off. My debts will get out of control and I'll lose everything."

"Hold on. Let's go back to what I was saying. You serve everyone else day in and day out but yourself. You're making life for all those around you better and richer. When do you get to pay attention to YOU?"

"I don't get it. What do you expect me to *do*?"

"I can't answer that for you. Figure out what will make you happy and go after that with all you've got. Right now, everyone else is benefiting off you, from you . . . *except* you. Get what I'm saying?"

"Sort of, but I still don't know what I'm supposed to *do*."

"Your bills will always be with you until you die. And when you die, like my momma says, you're going to your grave by yourself. You can't take your money with you and you can't take your bills with you. Don't be a slave to your debt. Take responsibility for it, but don't be so afraid of changing directions that you stay in this sorry victim mode forever."

As soon as I said the word *victim*, she started defending herself, which I expected. This is exactly the kind of thinking that's out there. That debt is bad. That debt cannot lead to riches. And that when debt happens, you become a victim. You're blocked out.

"Face it," I said. "You feel like the world is out to get you. You've got all this stuff to deal with that makes life seem unfair. But that victim mentality isn't going to get you anywhere. Neither will blaming the bills and the job. This job may pay your debts *in the long run*, but how long do you want to wait to feel good about yourself? You're young and smart. But you're stuck.

It's time for a 'radical sabbatical.' I'll be honest, it's very difficult to dig yourself out of debt just by working with what you have. I know there are lots of books out there about debt management, but in reality the concept is a lot of wishful thinking. When you're in debt, you don't have the money. Period. You have to invest in a chance and take a dare. Don't stay at a job for any reason other than a passion for what you're doing. It's obvious you're not passionate about how you spend your days now, and it's not even paying your bills."

Shanel let my words sink in, and I kept going. What I had to say would not fully match the conventional wisdom I know Shanel was familiar with and was loyally adhering to. It was going to take a little effort on my part to get her to see things my way.

"Forget about the debt for now. Let me put it this way: How would it feel *not* to have to go to work tomorrow? What if you could wake up at any time you wished? What if you didn't owe anybody *anything*?" I caught her smiling. She must have felt good for a split-second. "Okay, now notice how you feel right this instant," I said quickly. "You look like you just got a taste of heaven. I simply gave you permission to imagine not having to go to work tomorrow, and it affected you deep down inside. Look, too many people remain at jobs they hate for the wrong reasons, like health insurance or some other 'benefit.' They end up existing and not living. Right now you're just existing."

"I don't have a choice. You heard me: I have too many responsibilities," she said.

"That's where you're wrong. You have all the choices in the world. The same drive and freedom of choice that got you here—the same ambition and right to decide you wanted to buy a house and be an insurance agent—is the same drive and freedom of choice that will get you whatever else you want. Or, in the case of your unpaid bills, what you *don't* want. No one is holding the remote control to you—not your bills and certainly not your job. You've always had that control through the decisions you've made. So what you decide to do today changes where you are tomorrow. I'm not telling you to quit your job this week. That's not what I mean by radical. I'm asking you to change your attitude and your focus. Stop feeling sorry for yourself and you'll be amazed at what you can see in your future. The steps you need to take will follow."

I then encouraged her to think about what she was truly passionate about and what she could see herself doing if money wasn't a problem. It took a while to get her mind off her debt, but eventually she opened up. Her favorite show was *Law & Order*. Her favorite books were legal mysteries. She also mentioned that she felt "totally in her element" when her job required anything related to the law. Clearly the legal field made her light up inside.

"Why don't you go to law school?" I suggested.

"Are you kidding me? That's too expensive!"

"You're still not getting what I'm saying. You work a job right now that you hate and that may never make you happy. Your debt is controlling your life as well as your way of thinking. Just because you have debt doesn't mean you can't move forward and make things happen. Debt is not your destiny. Lots of people see debt as The End. That's a big lie. Step around the debt for now. If you take the dare and follow your dream, the debt will take care of itself. You don't have to have zero debt to be rich—I'll explain that later. For now just put the debt problems aside and pay attention to what you want to do."

I gave her some homework, which included checking out the application process for law school. I also told her that if she had to sell her house to help pay the tuition, that would be okay; she'd be able to afford a better home with a better mortgage plan later on and really reap the benefits of home ownership. Right now her home wasn't an asset; it was an obstacle.

By the time we stepped outside to go home, it was almost midnight. "Now you see, we're leaving my office in the middle of the night. I'm laughing. I have no stress. And I'm happy. Only a fool works himself to death for somebody else. I tell people that no matter what they're doing, even if they have to take a pay cut, if they can go home and smile at the end of the day—and their necessities are taken care of—that's what life is about."

For someone like Shanel, taking the dare may mean going back to school. For others it might be taking a second job or internship, or starting a business from home that's in the direction of a dream. Still, for a few people the first dare simply can be

---

Are you happy at the end of the day? If your answer is no, then you're not taking enough chances. Invest in a chance. If you don't take that dare, then you'll always be playing it safe . . . and safe is not going to get you to where you want to be. **Safe will not provide safety in the long run**.

opening up the mind and seeing things from a different perspective and identifying opportunities that are staring you in the face. Which is what happened one night to a man named Rich Schmelzer when he came home from work one day to find his family dressing up in their funky-retro shoes.

Forewarning: The story I'm about to tell isn't about luck. When I first heard it, I knew I would have to retell it, because no one had talked about the scary moments these people had to overcome to achieve their success. Remember, I'm a cold-blooded realist, so I always find the facts behind the fairy tale.

FROM CRAFTS TO CORPORATION

When Rich Schmelzer, the father of three young girls, watched his wife, Sheri, help their girls accessorize their Croc shoes with buttons and baubles that were lying around the house, he got an idea—maybe this was something that could catch on. So he and Sheri went out and bought little charms—peace signs, happy faces, hearts, and rhinestones—at craft stores and glued them onto cuff links. Then they stuck the cuff links into their children's Crocs and sent them off to school. (If you're not familiar with Croc shoes, you don't have to go far to find them. They are all-purpose casual shoes that resemble gardening shoes, and they took off in 2003. If you use your imagination they might look like crocodiles, which is how they got their name.)

Once their girls started wearing their dressed-up footwear in public, orders began rolling in. Jibbitz, what they called their homemade accessories as well as the company, quickly took over the family's basement. The Schmelzers did what naturally came next and launched a Web site. After just two weeks, they were overwhelmed with requests for Jibbitz of all shapes and sizes. Stores caught on and began ordering hundreds at a time. Within twelve months, Jibbitz were being sold in more than 3,000 stores, and the Schmelzers had moved from the basement to a huge warehouse. Eventually the buzz reached the founder of Crocs himself, and a little over a year after making their first Jibbitz, Sheri and Rich struck an awesome deal that had the potential to bring in $20 million. Twenty million for plastic charms filling holes!

That's the shorthand version of the story. It highlights all the highs of this family's wildly successful experience. Too good to be true? Watch out for the word *luck* when it crosses your mind. It's tempting to see this story as one about chance or accident, and you know I don't believe in luck. Let's consider the dares this family had to take along the way. The first one was daring to invest in dozens of plastic charms and cuff links. (And the kids dared to wear them to school, hoping their shoes would catch on as being cool instead of dumb.) Rich, the family breadwinner, was in the computer industry and had been struggling to get his fledgling software company off the ground. He did have an entrepreneurial spark, but shoe charms? Think about how serious a dare it was to steal time away from his "real job" to play with glue and trinkets fit for feet on rubber shoes. When he told his colleagues that he was going to spend more time at home with his family and their favorite shoes and snap-on accessories, they must have wondered, What's he *doing*? What's he *thinking*?

The next dare came when Rich and Sheri tapped their home's equity for cash to fuel the growing business. They also got their parents working on the makeshift assembly line that they set up in the basement. Granny and Gramps were sticking charms on cuff links over long hours through the weekends, too. But the dares only continued to get bigger and scarier. Busting out of their home's seams, they stepped up to a 12,000-square-foot office and warehouse. They outsourced manufacturing to Asia. And then the most daunting dare of all came when they agreed to take $10 million from Crocs for their start-up company, which would then operate as a subsidiary, plus $10 million more *if* they hit earnings targets. A gamble?

No, not a gamble. A dare to be successful. While the Schmelzers did take on some debt, including a loan on their house, it was the right kind of debt for the right kind of reasons. One of the most powerful aspects of this story is that it shows how you can piggyback on a product phenomenon. It's proof that you can turn crafts into a corporation without reinventing the wheel. We often think we have to come up with something brainy and complex to achieve success, but it's not true. If you think you have to become the next so-and-so or founder of such-and-such, you're wrong (and you haven't been listening to my message). I want you to be the next YOU. The Schmelzers did nothing more than start with an existing product they loved—the funny Croc shoes—and make it better with a simple accessory. There's not much brain chemistry in that.

THE WEALTHY SIDE OF DEBT

There is a significant difference between the types of debt that Shanel is facing and that of the Jibbitz founders. Shanel cannot invest in herself because she's paying everyone else; the Schmelzers on the other hand are paying into their dream every day—even at the risk of owing others. Worst-case scenario: They could lose their house and have more bills to pay. But so could Shanel, without even taking the dare. In fact, Shanel already has more bills to pay than she can handle.

What many people forget or just don't realize is that debt is a necessary step toward fortune. Let me repeat that: **Debt can get you on your way to wealth if used wisely.** You don't have to have zero debt to either 1) start building wealth, or 2) be rich. In fact, it would be *impossible* to become wealthy without the help of debt, which, by the way, includes credit.

I know this is contrary to popular thinking and conventional wisdom, but let me explain.

Millionaires and billionaires are richer on paper than they are at the bank. They own homes, income properties, stocks and bonds, companies, trademarks, patents, rights, and other assets

---

THE DEBT TRUTH:

You must **have debt** to get rich.
You must **use debt** to get rich.

that they can't whip out of their pocket to pay for food at the grocery store or a Saturday night out. They do carry debt—sometimes a lot of debt—in the form of mortgages, second mortgages, a line of credit, or a business loan or an education loan that they are paying back diligently over time. They try to stay away from high-interest credit cards or loans they know they cannot pay back according to terms. If you are dishing out cash that you really don't have to cover fees and finance charges on balances that never shrink, it's like splashing water out from a boat that is sinking faster than you can bail. At some point the boat's weight will take you down. Many of you already may have an understanding of this (or at least sense it from experience), but what you don't know is how to abandon ship and seek solid ground. The secret is to shrink the bad debt and attract the good debt. That's what will make you wealthy.

In the previous chapter you got an understanding of the different types of debt, and why not all debt is created equal. But unfortunately a lot of people don't have a healthy balance. Last year, for the first time ever recorded, Americans owed more money

---

REALITY CHECK: Sit down. Add up your credit card balances (let's leave out the mortgage for now). If the number is higher than $9,000, welcome to the club. The club of the average American family, that is. The good news: You can move on up to the wealthy club by doing one common-sensical thing: Start thinking in terms of missions and plans.

than they made. Household debt levels surpassed income by more than 8 percent, and consumer debt is now at a record $2.17 trillion. Homeowners in particular cashed out a whopping $431 billion in equity during 2005 to help keep up with the rising cost of living (including paying for things like new cars, vacations, and plasma televisions—not a budding company like Jibbitz).

DEBTS WITH A MISSION AND A PLAN

Another important difference between Shanel and the Schmelzers is how they approached their debt. The Schmelzers have a clear plan for paying off what they owe through the success of their company. As revenues increase over time, they will generate more power to pay down loans and lines of credit. But what does Shanel have to get rid of her debts? Her debts are largely "spent"—they are *lie*-abilities. They have little to no value and cannot be used to invest in her future. They've made everyone else rich (i.e., her mortgage lender, her car financer, the credit card companies, and so on) *but* her. She's been lying to herself, thinking all of her hard work and dedication will pay off. It won't. Not at the speed she's going. She has no equity in her home and no strategy for paying that all back in her lifetime. What she does have, frankly, is a "plan" to work her butt off (for someone else's gain) and stay miserable. She barely can make it as it is. That's why she's so terrified to quit her job. That's why she has to take that gigantic dare to consider her passion for law and go back to school.

I get a lot of questions about credit cards, which carry some of the most troubling forms of debt today. They cause a lot of heartache and sleepless nights. Shanel's credit card balances rang in second after her mortgage on her list of worries. To make my point about what it means to have a mission and plan for wealth through good debt, ask yourself this question: What do you use a credit card for? To go shopping for weekend clothes? That's not a mission and a plan. Or do you use it to pay for an outfit that you need to nail a job interview? Now *that's* a mission and a plan.

I never had a chance to get into credit card debt. How could I? I had to think cash before credit. I was a preteen when I started my own company. I was too young to legally apply for a credit card! I couldn't even sign my name alone to open a bank account. But eventually, by the time I could qualify for credit, I already had learned how to think like a venture capitalist. Do you know how venture capitalists treat dollars and cents? Like Mother Duck counts her ducklings, watching money as if it were a living, breathing creature. To others, however, money isn't alive. It's meaningless for the most part. And electronic banking has completely taken the feelings out of the transaction. Debit. Click. Debit. Click. Debit. Debit. **Debt.** Paper money has become obsolete. I laughed out loud when someone recently summed up the prevailing attitude toward money: "If I owe the bank $15,000, that's my responsibility. If I owe the bank $50,000, that's the *bank's* problem!"

After I laughed out loud, I felt sad. People don't have a clue how much money it's costing them in interest and finance charges. They also don't have a clue about how long it could take to pay off a large balance. If they can pay the monthly minimum, they think they're doing okay. When the numbers on the balance sheet go through the roof, panic turns into passivity. People lose sight of what that bottom-line number really means, and their normal reaction is to blame someone else for it. *How the heck did I get into so much debt? When did this happen?* That's when they begin to resist. They resist because they can't mentally handle The Number, so they tune out and check out. Now it's the "bank's problem."

If everyone thought like a venture capitalist, there would be no credit card debt. The first thing these guys do is learn to buy with a purpose—with a mission and a plan—whether they are using cash or credit. Imagine if you did that every time you were going to buy something. I bet you'd never acquire bad debt.

Let's play with this. Picture yourself walking into a car dealership. Your car is only two years old, but you've had your eyes on the newer, sportier model that just came out. You really love this car and can see yourself driving it today. You're thinking of all the ways to make it work—to turn in your current car and then sign a new loan for the new car, which will cost a lot more money. It will put you further in the hole each month, but what the heck. You get to drive a beautiful car. Your emotions have already taken over. You'll figure out how to pay for it later.

Stop! Let's apply the Mission Test. What's your goal here? The only one I can think of isn't really a goal at all. It's to look good when you're driving around town and have the latest technology at your fingertips. What's the plan for paying for this goal? Going into more debt that will have little to no future value. It's a *lie-*

> If you have lie-abilities, which are those financial liabilities that have little to no future value, then you need to think **cash** before **credit**.
>
> Remember, it's easier to increase cash flow than to decrease consumer credit debt.

ability. You don't have a plan. You're lying to yourself if you think you do.

Granted, we all have lie-abilities. Once in a while we need to cut back on the things we could probably live without but that we think will make us happier. You may want to eat at a fancy restaurant from time to time. You may not want to give up your weekly iPod downloads or monthly spa treatments. You don't need to cut yourself off all lie-abilities; you just have to start being smart about keeping your missions and goals in mind. I believe we all have a gut instinct that can distinguish between what's survival and what's luxury. It's common sense but not common practice. Go with that instinct.

"Suitable" Credit

In addition to my exposure to venture-capitalist thinking early on, part of my internal programming is also related to the fact I came from the projects, where my momma's triple jobs still didn't make ends meet. Money represented safety. Each dollar was equal to an option. The more options we had, the greater our security. I still value money like this. It needs to be cared for. Whether it's disguised as credit or pulled from an ATM, money is money.

Let me tell you another story about debt. This one is about that other lie that says credit is bad, and that only poor people have to rely on credit because they don't have the money today.

If you haven't already noticed, I like to wear suits. I *love* expensive suits. I wear them just about every day. Over the years, as I started making more public appearances, designers would approach me and ask me to wear their suits. I was honored at first, and I enjoyed promoting other people's brands that I liked for a while. But then one day as I was answering someone's question about which designer I was wearing, it dawned on me, "Why can't these be *my* suits?" Why should I wear somebody else's suits when I could make my own and profit from them? How cool is that? I'm not the only one who loves suits. There are an awful lot of other people out there who are just like me who spend a lot of money on their everyday clothes. So I contacted someone I knew in the fashion industry who was a brilliant sketcher and specialty tailor with more than thirteen years of experience. I simply asked him if I could invest in his company. I could offer him a capital boost and the means for launching an entire product line into retail stores. As soon as we started talking about the logistics—how we'd find a manufacturer to produce the suits and sell them to retailers—we got really excited. It was a done deal. I was in the suit business.

Now, I ask you, how do you think we pay for the materials and manufacturing of our suits? Do we take out $100 bills from our wallets or write large checks? Of course not. We have a huge line of credit with the company that supplies our fabrics. This allows us to have our suits made without having to fully pay for their manufacturing until we start selling them. If we don't bring in money (i.e., sell the suits), we have to pay back that debt, plus any penalty fees for not meeting our terms of the contract. The agreement we have with our supplier spells out when they get paid; we have to pay for the suits whether or not we sell them. But typically the agreement is set up so we can sell enough suits in time to start paying back what we owe the fabric company. And eventually we make more money in sales than we need to pay for those suits. And there is the profit.

This is how it works in much of the business world. Everything in business is about credit and debt. You go into short-term debt for a long-term profit. The printing industry works this way, too. A magazine, for example, will print $1 million in magazines—paid entirely on credit with a printer that does all the physical manufacturing of the product—and then as those magazines sell for profit, the loan gets paid back. It would be as if you had a 300-page magazine to produce, and you walk into a Kinko's with your pages on a CD all laid out and ready to go. You need help in transforming your content onto glossy pages in color—printing, binding, and packaging the actual magazines for shipment. The cost? A lot. But you know you can cover that cost through your sales, and then make bundles more. You need to reach an agreement with Kinko's so you can get your magazines produced, start selling them, and *then* pay the bill.

Pretend for a moment that you want to be the next Donald

Trump. You dream of creating a few of the world's most luxurious destinations, and you need more than a few bucks. Way more than a few bucks. You actually need *millions*. Doable? Well, that's what Steve Wynn needed when he had a vision for his casino resorts in Las Vegas—to the tune of $700 million. Empires don't get built on cash. They get built on *credit*.

So now you're wondering whether you should run out and put your business idea on your Visa or MasterCard. After all, I just said empires get built on credit. And a few pages ago I said debt creates wealth. Hold your fire. Dare to be successful, but don't dare to be reckless and unrealistic. People want me to say it's okay to rely on credit cards for investment purposes. Like I said in the previous chapter, it can be tempting to use a $5,000 credit line to help pay for a start-up business, or even living expenses while you get your business up and running. A good idea?

First, clean up bad debt. Second, start noticing *why* you access credit and loans. And third, make sure you plug in a mission and a plan. Caution: What I'm about to say may concur with what you'll hear in most money-management circles. I don't care how many credit cards you have; while having fewer cards may make you *think* you can better control your debts, it's all relative. Get real about what you can handle. And remember: Stay away from

---

REALITY CHECK—TAKE TWO: Does everything go as planned? No way. You only hear about the stories of people who hit it big. That's why I'm careful about how much credit I use with my budding suit company.

consolidating down to one card. You are better off managing three or four credit cards than squeezing your purchasing power down to one card that you use for everything. I want you to overcome your credit card debt *despite* the number of credit cards you have. I want you to learn how to manage your debt *despite* the bottom-line number.

Again, there are plenty of resources out there to help you work step by step to manage consumer debt. (Refer to the Resource Directory on my Web site for leads.) Don't forget: While you're getting your debt under control, you must look at the bigger picture. You must also move beyond the books and the tutorials.

Remember: Have a mission. Have a plan.

ATTACH ACTION TO YOUR MISSION AND PLANS

Missions and plans are only the beginning. A recipe for chicken pot pie will just sit there unless you get cooking. Ingredients alone won't change your life. They require action. You need a chef. Your debts won't shift from the bad side to the good side until you attach a mission and a goal to them, and then get cooking. The same is true of success. You can't achieve it until you attach a mission and goal, and then put it in the oven! This is the bigger picture I'm talking about.

One of the first set of "ingredients" I ever had was a mission to become a talk-show host. But here was the problem: I had no idea how to put the recipe together because I knew nothing about being a talk-show host or even landing a gig. At the time I was fifteen years old and living in Las Vegas. I had an idea for a radio program geared toward teenagers. So I grabbed the Yellow Pages and called radio stations to ask questions. Eventually I learned that I had to speak to a program director. Those were the guys who would listen to my pitch, which was: "Teenscope: the 911 and 411 reality teen talk show." Long story short, I was rejected across the board. Across Las Vegas. I even went off (after someone recommended it) and produced a pilot to demonstrate a test sampling of what my intended show would be like, hoping *that* would land me a deal somewhere. But it didn't. No one wanted to take my show.

While some people might have given up at this juncture and felt like a loser, I thought, "I'm meeting with the wrong person." My contacts were coming up with every reason under the sun to say no to me, so I believed I was having the wrong conversation. It wasn't about me or my show. It was about *them*. That's when I decided to buy my own time and produce my own show— another subject area about which I knew absolutely nothing. So I plunged myself completely into "doing the knowledge," learning how to make that happen. I spoke with sales directors and went after advertisers; I wanted my show to be so good that somebody would buy it. (Note right here that I wasn't throwing credit cards at producers to pay for my show. I still didn't have them! I was forced to get crafty with the big picture in mind.) I wrote up my own media kit, sought sponsors, joined the city's chamber of commerce (of which I later became a board member), started networking, and introduced myself to as many people who might propel me forward as I could. This wasn't a forty-eight-hour effort. This took *months*, close to a year. But it was what I wanted and it was part of my mission. The process was thrilling. I had a purpose. And I was confident that my ship eventually would come in.

Bingo. The car company Saturn surfaced and offered to sponsor my show completely if I broadcasted live from various Saturn dealerships in the Vegas area. The company wanted to get parents to buy Saturns for their teenage children. It was a mutually beneficial relationship, and it was a magical moment for me. The Teenscope Youth AM/FM interactive teen talk show was born. From there I went on to do bigger things in radio and beyond. What if I hadn't been persistent and determined at the start? What if I had given up? I might not have arrived at the place where I am today.

By now you know I hate the saying about being at the right place at the right time. You have to be *everywhere* all the time, letting people know that you exist. It's about doing, not talking or

---

Thoughts are exhausting. Thoughts will make you sleepy before you even get out of bed. Anxiety and stress are paralyzing. I call it the "analysis paralysis."

You may be thinking too much.

You sit and think all day—caught up with debt—until you do . . . nothing.

Attach **action** to your thoughts and see what happens.

thinking. This is exactly why I insist on moving beyond conversation to accomplishment. You have to do the thinking, but then the *doing*. The doing will get you out of bad debt. The doing will bring you opportunities for good debt, which will then pay you multiple times over.

The doing will make you a success again and again.

Be a Cold-blooded Realist

I'm a cold-blooded realist. The *doing* is easier said than done. If doing were so easy, then I wouldn't see the same people coming back to hear me speak for a second or third time. They would have taken my message and implemented it right away, and not needed more help or inspiration from me. What gives? This goes back to why I wrote this chapter: debt. Of all the things that can fuel our fears and consume our thoughts, debt ranks up there at number one. We saw this with Shanel. Her debt and "responsibilities" were taking up a lot of space in her mind and spirit. Debt crushes our courage to see things differently, to take that dare.

I'll never get out of credit card debt.

I'll never fully own my home.

*I'll never leave this job or change careers . . . **because of my debt**.*

*I'll never work for myself . . . **because of my debt**.*

*I'll never get unstuck . . . **because of my debt**.*

Sound familiar? Well, you're right. You won't unless you do something radical. You must do the dare *in spite of* your debt if you're ever going to see a change and come out a winner.

I DARE YOU!

No one is born running. You had to be carried before you could crawl. Eventually you walked, then ran . . . and then hopped on a bicycle with training wheels. After graduating to a two-wheeler, you drove. At that point, the sky was the limit. Nothing could stop you then, and nothing should be stopping you now.

It's amazing what you can accomplish when you don't know what you *can't* do yet. Behavioral scientists tell us we were born with two primal fears: the fear of loud noises and the fear of falling. That's it. What about the fear of failure? The fear of making a mistake? The fear of rejection? And, as we just saw, the fear of debt. Those, my friends, are fears created by society. In fact, any other fears you can think of are lies. Pretty crazy.

This explains why we fear things we shouldn't, like going out and taking that dare. When we come up with an idea, we may hear our inner voice immediately say, "This hasn't been done yet, so it probably won't work. Otherwise it already would have been done if it was a good idea." Or "I can't afford to test this idea. I'm already being chased for money. I can't make my debt any worse." With thoughts like these, we quickly lose momentum and come to a screeching halt. We stay in a cycle of bad debt and misery.

Also consider this: If an idea doesn't work out, does that mean *you* are not a success? No. It just means that the idea didn't work, pure and simple. You learn. You move on. You test your next idea. That's what I did when I hunted down a yes for my show in Vegas. That's what I was urging Shanel to do. Being an insurance agent wasn't working. It was an idea and a life for somebody else. It was time to say "Next!"

Remember, you can't win if you don't play. Open any dictionary and look up the word *failure*. Somewhere buried among the false definitions is its true meaning: *not doing; neglect or omission; nonperformance of a duty*.

Everything you want is on the other side of fear.

SHANEL'S PLAN AND STRATEGY

Let's go back to Shanel. You're probably wondering what happened to her. Did she quit her job and go back to school?

Hold up! Not so fast. Shanel is still planning her transition. While her gut may be telling her what she *should* be doing, there is still resistance to taking action. When I checked in on her progress a few weeks after our initial talk, she appeared confused and unmotivated. So I asked her more questions. It was time for Round 2.

"What does success mean to you?"

She didn't have an answer, saying something like *Being happy at the end of the day, like I've contributed something to the world, I guess; and I'm not bogged down by thoughts about money.* I didn't think that was good enough. It didn't pinpoint her ideals and passions. It was too general and bland. She had no purpose. No wonder she wasn't moving forward with a positive attitude.

To some success is all about money. If you can bring in a million dollars a year, you're "wealthy." To others, success is all about getting the perfect job, or being in the perfect marriage, or living the perfect life. If you feel "perfect"—whatever that might be—you're successful. There are other ways humans have come to define success, but one thing is true: Success must be defined and a goal must be set before it can be achieved. Everyone wants to be happy; that's a no-brainer. But if you make that your definition of success, how do you attach goals to it? It's too broad. It's too vague. Sorry, but it's wishy-washy. Same goes for making "success" your goal in a vacuum. Success, as we've seen, should be viewed as an attitude, just like happiness.

"Your debt won't suddenly disappear on its own without a plan, right?" I asked Shanel. She nodded slowly in semiagreement. "Well, success won't spontaneously *appear* without a plan, either. So you need a checkup from the neck up."

This was an important lesson that Shanel needed to learn. She didn't have a specific definition of success that matched her needs, wants, and desires. Nor did she have a clear mission and a plan for achieving that success.

I told her to think about reaching a goal in terms of driving to the nearest gas station when the tank was running near empty. "How could you possibly get to the gas station taking the shortest route if you haven't clearly defined that path? Would you just drive all around the neighborhood hoping it would jump out in front of you and save your day? Of course not. You would sit down and locate that station before you even got into your car and started the engine."

That's how life is. Why would you go through your days wasting precious time, effort, and other resources without defining your actual goal? The question may sound elementary, but many

---

The Three Questions

---

1. What comes easy to you but harder to others?
2. What would you do for years even if you didn't get paid for it?
3. How can you be of service—how can you give back to others and your community?

---

people, like Shanel, live this way and wonder why they're never really happy. And why they also live in that dark side of debt their whole lives. I pushed Shanel to reflect seriously on what would make her genuinely happy. I told her to envision herself with a law degree. I also asked her to see herself living in her dream home and being able to pay all her bills in full each month with plenty of money left over. Once she could visualize this, she could begin to pinpoint her destination and map out her route with a set of goals to take her there. I wrote out my three-question test, which she had done once before when we talked initially, but I told her to go through it again. Just to be sure.

"But don't worry about figuring out *all* the goals," I said to her. "Just the first one is fine for now. You'll figure out the rest as you go along. You don't create your destiny. You *discover* it."

We often look at our ultimate goal—our dreamy final destination—as impossible to get to. After all, who wants to look one hundred miles in the distance when the first few miles look challenging enough? Does a first-year med student agonize over performing open-heart surgery? Certainly not. This is why it's helpful to look at smaller portions of the goal, the baby steps you take one at a time. For Shanel, who after answering the three questions maintained her goal of being a lawyer, her baby step was to start looking at a calendar to schedule her application process and eventually leave her company. In the meantime, while still bringing in some income, she'd focus on paying down her credit cards, and possibly sell her house.

The thought of making these changes was intimidating. But I knew that her sense of purpose would soon override the fears, which is what Shanel craved deep down. I'm confident she will find what she's looking for if she has the courage to move forward and keep going.

Your idea of success may be to teach small children to read and write, or to lead a football team to a national championship. Your idea of success may be to own a multimillion-dollar business, or work your way to a high level of management in a multibillion-dollar corporation. Whatever your definition of success is, it must be the goal for your life.

Let your passion pull you forward. Work around your debt and eventually the debt will work itself out. Don't let the lies and fears cover up the truth. Always remember that debt is not your destiny. It's not an ends to a means. It's a means to an end—when used with missions, plans, and action.

I'LL HAVE THE STEAK, PLEASE

One of my favorite anecdotes I like to tell at speaking appearances starts by asking how many people in the audience have dogs; many people raise their hands. I ask how many of them like dogs; again, many hands go up. Then I ask this question: *Do dogs like bones?* I turn the mike over to face the audience and wait for a resounding YES. After the response, I deliver the punch line: *No, dogs don't like bones, they like steak. They settle for bones because that's all they can get!*

What are you settling for in life?

If I were you, I'd go after the steak.

An idea is never given to you without you being given the power to make it reality. You must, nevertheless, suffer for it.

— RICHARD BACH

6

The Google and Gates Lie

Lie: I have to be super-smart and invent something the world relies on to be rich.

Truth: Intelligence, wit, and inventiveness will only get you so far. Big things are born from satisfying small niches.

Stories like those about Microsoft, Apple, and Google are part thrilling, part depressing. They make it hard not to believe that you must create something über-spectacular for the world's people to soak up virtually every day and demand updates year after year. And this isn't just about technology and computers. The same goes for all kinds of "inventions," including things like the Harry Potter franchise, the Phat Farm and Def Jam empires, and food kingdoms like McDonald's, Coca-Cola, and Heinz.

Sure, it would be nice to become the next Bill Gates, Russell Simmons, J. K. Rowling, or Google guys (founders Larry Page and Sergey Brin). But let's face it: They already have covered that territory and there are millions of others out there who have been successful without taking the same path. So don't panic. As

I've been telling you, it's never been easier to access information, self-educate, break traditional rules, start a small business, and climb your own corporate ladder. Traditional modes of wealth creation are outdated. Attending top schools and getting degrees, for example, are no longer surefire paths to success (*Time* magazine named Gates, who dropped out of Harvard two years shy of getting his degree, one of the most influential people of the twentieth century). Neither is inventing a gadget the world is waiting for (sorry, Mr. Gates). Thinking too big can be overwhelming and paralyzing. It can also leave you disheartened and full of anxiety, thinking, "I can't ever get to that point. That's just too much work. I'm so far behind. Besides, someone else will beat me to it."

REALITY CHECK: Success is no longer measured by being #1 or #2 in a field—it's in finding a niche and creating something new or improving an existing product or service (the proverbial "build a better mousetrap" idea—a cliché, but it works!).

You don't necessarily have to think big, as in Microsoft or Google big. You don't have to become the next media and entertainment magnate like Sean "Diddy" Combs or Rupert Murdoch. Mind you, even they started small and took sequential steps. They didn't just land in their shoes overnight. Do you know who Shigeru Miyamoto is? I'll give you a hint: He found a niche decades ago when he created (the now iconic) Mario and Donkey Kong. Today he's celebrated as the father of modern video gaming and is perfecting his latest hit—the Nintendo Wii system. As a young boy, Miyamoto loved to draw, paint pictures, and explore the landscape surrounding his house. It's no surprise that his creative interests, which included a fascination for discovering hidden caves, lakes, and other natural features, spawned the popular Legend of Zelda. Of course, this meant he had to put his interests and talents to work, which is exactly what he did when he arranged a meeting with the head of Nintendo of Japan in 1977. He was hired as a staff artist and became an apprentice in the planning department, and the rest is history.

When two twentysomething regular guys decided to create a means for people to watch and share original videos worldwide through the Web (i.e., YouTube), never in their wildest dreams did they think their niche idea would generate more than 70 million thirsty viewers a day gobbling up its content and be worth $1.65 billion in less than two years. Talk about going from mini-movies to mass market.

Today's niches are tomorrow's big things, period. You simply have to think small and take baby steps. And that first step only requires that you have an attitude that rejects this nasty lie and respects the truth.

THE GOOGLE AND GATES TRUTH:

Intelligence, wit, and inventiveness will only get you so far. Big things are born from satisfying small niches, and no idea is too dumb that you can't get millions of people to buy into it.

NO PHD REQUIRED

You can make money at everything and in everything. We often don't realize the simplicity in ideas and concepts.

REALITY CHECK: Ideas in action make money, nothing else.

Calvin Coolidge was right: Nothing is more common than unsuccessful men with talent, unrewarded genius is almost a proverb, and the world is full of educated derelicts.

Just look around you. Everything that we touch and admire or use is something that someone has created—and that you likely bought. Entrepreneurship is all about the laws of supply and demand. You find the demand, and fill the void with supplies. It doesn't necessarily have to be a tangible thing or a sage piece of advice based on years of formal schooling, as in the case of professionals such as lawyers, doctors, scientists, engineers, PhDs, and the like. It can be your expertise based on experience alone in an industry you've been a part of for a long time. (Note how close those two words are: *expert*-ise and *experi*ence.) It can be a widget you craftily whip up in your basement or a secret family recipe you bake up and package beautifully to market. People have made successful businesses out of selling water. And there are plenty of people who

simply have the idea but not all the critical know-how to follow through on their ideas on their own. Those types find
others with whom to partner or hire and make the idea come
alive—and with a greater chance of success. All entrepreneurs
confront unfamiliar territory in the journey, and that's when
you reach out to others.

Granted, sometimes it does take a little more schooling to
fine-tune your ideas and do the knowledge completely. That's
okay. I'm not putting down formal education—my point is that
education is very important, be it formal or informal. But degrees alone don't make the money—YOU make the money based
on your bright ideas and how well you can execute them. YOU
must take whatever education and degrees you receive and do
something with them. Everyone's path will be different. You can,
for example, get an idea going and educate yourself as you see fit,
especially once you know you've got something that is working.
Institutions today are more flexible in giving you the education
you need, so you don't have to lock yourself into a traditional setting for multiple semesters and be distracted from focusing on
your ideas. On the other hand, some careers do require formal
schooling. If being a lawyer or architect channels your passions
and skills, then you would do well to finish up that schooling
quickly rather than drag it out endlessly. This also will keep your
costs down and allow you to branch out sooner to use your degree in a variety of opportunities, maybe even establishing your
own firm.

NATURALLY BORN
ENTREPRENEURS

Is there an entrepreneurial gene? Can you be born with or without it?

If there's one place in the world where people are born natural entrepreneurs, it's in third-world countries. Think about it: If you are born where you must get crafty for the sake of your own survival—to find the basics like food, water, and shelter—you are going to awaken those entrepreneurial spirits automatically. People who immigrate to the United States typically have an "I can do anything" mentality. Why? Because they are coming to a place that, relatively speaking, offers limitless opportunities and few, if any, obstacles. Sure, not everybody in the United States would say their life is peachy keen and without challenges, but the struggles many immigrants endure in their home countries pale in comparison to what they find when they land in the "Great USA"—even if they arrive with no money, no credit, little experience, and no job lined up.

I wholeheartedly believe that we all have the potential to be entrepreneurs. It's encoded in our cells as humans struggling to survive on this planet for millennia. Picture our caveman ancestors who were met with life-threatening circumstances every day. They didn't have the luxuries we take advantage of today. Those who were courageous enough to venture farther out from the settled territories were the most risk-taking entrepreneurs. They sought the same things today's entrepreneurs seek—adventure, newness, autonomy, and perhaps a better life.

But what separates the immigrant mentality from those who are born ahead of the game is attitude. There's an old story about a shoe company that in the late 1800s sent two salesmen to Africa to evaluate the potential of the market there. The first one writes back: "Nobody here wears shoes . . . useless market." Soon thereafter arrives the missive from the other: "Nobody here wears shoes . . . fantastic market." Notice the difference in perspective? The second guy sees a gold mine—opportunity galore—and is excited not only about selling shoes but teaching the inhabitants how and why to wear them. He's also thankful to the company for sending him. The first guy feels defeated and sees nothing but a U-turn. He is unhappy that he got chosen to go to Africa.

Two different mind-sets. One market. Which man will make money?

It's far too easy to overlook what someone else sees clearly. As Americans we often don't listen to our innate entrepreneurial spirit because we are born with so much more, and we are surrounded with so much more. Some of us may think we come from a place of lack, but the majority of us are not born on the streets. And we don't have to beg for food on a filthy or unpaved street corner, nor do we have to travel endless miles for fresh water. I wish every American would acknowledge and embrace their inner rabbit-and-fox mentality in the way that immigrants do. The rabbit outruns the fox because it's running for its life. The fox is only running for its dinner. Now I ask you, how hungry are you? Are you running for your dinner or running for your life?

Last year when I was in St. Thomas I came across a man with a donkey dressed up as a woman with makeup and light clothing.

He was a hit with tourists, and the man made a killing day after day. Every time someone asked to have a photograph taken with the donkey, he kindly accepted payment. When you visit poorer countries, you'll likely find people peddling whatever they can to squeak out a living and feed their families. These are entrepreneurs at work. Imagine what they could do if given the opportunities we have here in the United States.

When Ablade Odoi-Atsem immigrated to the United States from Ghana in 1984, he brought with him a yearning to be an entrepreneur and found his own company someday. He spent the next fifteen years gaining experience in the construction industry, providing project management and cost-control services, before founding Odoi Associates, Inc., in 1998. During his grooming years in the United States, he educated himself in building technology and completed postgraduate work in finance and international business so he could maximize the skills he needed to run a successful business. His goal was to establish a company that could provide a complete range of building services with superior attention to quality and customer care, which, for all intents and purposes, is like building that better mousetrap. Odoi-Astem admits that he had to max out his personal credit card to get his start-up going, and he credits much of his success to selecting the right people to work with, all of whom brought additional critical skills and knowledge to the table. This is something important to bear in mind. When you require some know-how or skills to enhance the execution of your ideas, don't be afraid to snap them up from other people. At first, you usually have to rely on your own sets of skills first and wear all the hats.

But at a later point, you must open up to others who can broaden your horizons, help you reach more customers, and increase sales. The expertise of others will also help you to spot trends and forthcoming changes in technology and your industry, and help you to better adapt and evolve with the times.

Today Odoi-Astem's company is a leading force in the industry, specializing in government contracts. At this writing, Odoi Associates is an $8.2 million venture with sights on expanding globally in the private sector. Last year it ranked #96 on the Hot 500 of *Entrepreneur* magazine's top fast-growth businesses.

There's no shortage of magazines catering to entrepreneurs looking for ideas and inspiration and step-by-step guidance on many details. The next time you pass a newsstand, check out *Entrepreneur, Inc., Wired, SmartMoney, Fast Company, Business 2.0, Fortune*, and any others that interest you. In 2006, the Small Business Administration launched "Mind Your Own Business" at www.mindyourownbusiness.org to help young entrepreneurs go from start-up idea to revenue. If you don't think you fall under the "young" category (i.e., you're not a teenager) then try the traditional site at www.sba.gov. Also look for trade magazines that cover your particular area of excellence. Some examples you might not have heard of: *Marie Claire Idees, Fine Woodworking, Paper Crafts*, and *Knitter's*. If you don't find what you're looking for at your local newsstand, try Amazon.com. There you can search by exact subject. You'll find my *Prominent* magazine available at newsstands and online at www.prominentmagazine.com—it's chock-full of ideas and words of wisdom to get you started.

Now, I ask you, can we trace Odoi-Astem's success back to luck or connections? No. Stardom? I don't think so. Wealth? Nope. Zero debt? Not really. What Odoi-Astem had was the spirit to become an entrepreneur, plus the drive, hustle, and ambition to see his dream come true.

HOW LONG IS YOUR TAIL?

The meaning of the concept of niche may not be obvious on the surface, so let's come to a clear understanding about what it means. Technically a niche is a small defined group of potential customers. Collectors of rare coins or toys constitute niche markets. Fans of competitive recreational sports like marathons and triathlons are a niche group. People who make a living remodeling and flipping homes represent a niche. Put simply, a niche is something that you have a knowledge and passion for. And if you are addressing a need for a product or service in that niche that is not being addressed by mainstream providers, you are a niche business. At one point eBay was catering to a niche market—people who enjoyed auctioning used goods; Match.com was a niche business—addressing single people who wanted help in finding dates; and even hip-hop record companies were once considered niche businesses—helping fellow brothers and sisters celebrate life and culture as they knew it. It comes as no surprise that the ability to find a niche hinges on knowing your audience and its needs. Or, shall we say, the ability to have a long tail.

In 2006 business writer Chris Anderson came out with a book called *The Long Tail: Why the Future of Business Is Selling Less of More*. It's a provocative treatise on the power of niches and how we now live in a world where bestsellers and smash hits don't mean what they used to mean. For example, we don't all watch the same TV shows anymore or read the same books. We don't all buy the same DVDs, music, toys, or household goods. The culprit? Access to endless options via the Internet with its limitless sellers and inventory. There used to be a finite number of shelves and space in brick-and-mortar stores. Now we can double-click our way to any store and market. The result, according to Anderson, is the "shattering of the mainstream into a zillion different cultural shards," creating "countless niches" that are market opportunities for those who cast a wide net and pay less attention to the search for a blockbuster.

Which brings me to explain to you the concept of a tail. Picture a bell curve. The area in the middle reflects those hits and top sellers—and lots of fifteen-mintues-of-famers at any given time. Now move away from the center and you'll see tails flanking the core. That's where millions of little shards lie. That's where lots of ideas meet lots of people on the fringes looking for your exact product or service. And because there is an infinite number of those perfect matches, there are multitudes of opportunities to come up with bestsellers, selling more items to fewer people. This bodes well for the entrepreneur who doesn't have a blockbuster idea brewing or who needs time to make their idea popular. You're better off having a long tail and finding a niche just big enough to keep you in business. Over time you can move toward that hearty center where you stand a chance of your idea becoming a mainstream bestseller.

But you may not even need to go there. You can very well be a hit out on the sidelines filling a single niche with several related products. This is how eBay millionaires have done it. The online auction site allows anyone to sell just about anything to the world at large. It's the quintessential umbrella over infinite niche markets, providing the ideal forum for making connections between buyers and sellers of you name it. Some people have even established successful businesses simply helping those buyers reach sellers, as in the case of Amy Mayer and Ellen Navarro, both twenty-five, who started an eBay drop-off store in Chicago called Express Drop. The niche? They sell items on consignment for individuals and high-end retailers. In 2006 they netted more than $1.4 million. Dan Glasure, thirty-one, took his passion for model trains (i.e., a niche) and began selling them plus their accessories on eBay to the tune of $2.5 million a year. His business's tail is long because while the number of people who are equally passionate about model trains and accessories is small and may be relatively finite, those same people keep coming back for more to keep their collections alive. James Anderson, twenty-eight, hawked enough iPod accessories and wizardry items, including swords, chalices, runes, and wands, in 2006 to make $2 million on the site. IPod accessories might be considered mainstream these days, but swords and chalices? Evidently enough people belong to this niche club and keep coming back for more. The combined value of Anderson's modest number of customers and the numerous quirky goods they guzzle up equals the sale of a single good sold once to many people.

Of course not everything is bought and sold online. There are just as many niches to fill in the real, offline world. Take Tina Wells, for instance. At twenty-six she's currently CEO of Buzz Marketing Group, a New York–based firm in its eleventh year working with companies to conduct market research on younger generations. She got started at sixteen when she began writing reviews on products of companies that target youth for the *New Girl Times*, a newspaper for young girls. Embracing her passion for fashion and her fascination with pop culture, Tina saw a huge disconnect between the desires of teens and the misdirected products and services offered by many companies. As soon she started submiting reviews and suggestions directly to these companies, she experienced an overwhelmingly positive response. Clearly she filled a deep crevasse, and today her company rakes in upward of $3.3 million annually, with kudos coming right and left from clients Nike, Dickies, Sony BMG, *Essence*, American Eagle, and NBC Universal. Now that's what I call a successful, celebrated individual who takes her talents and passions to the bank every day.

Another woman who addressed a niche is Monica Higgins, founder of Renovation Planners in Culver City, California. Her story proves that niches can be found in your own little neighborhood, which can then spread to other neighborhoods. In 2006 she noticed that local homeowners looked desperately in need of help in the remodeling process. She knew from experience that remodeling a home is a costly and often complicated, anxiety-driven process. So she set up a business to coordinate teams of designers, architects, contractors, and engineers to manage their remodels from concept to completion. Granted, Higgins is not a techy; she wears neither the engineer's nor the architect's hat. But she is excellent at handling the management details and making sure the process operates smoothly. What she offers homeowners is more than savings. Calling herself the passionate "hire-it-done" homeowner who helps people overcome "remodelitis"™ (a catchy term she has, in fact, trademarked), Higgins provides peace of mind and a more efficient system for people going through the remodeling process. By coordinating all the players involved, overseeing contractors, and staying on top of the over-all strategy, her company helps customers get to the finish line quicker and avoid costly changes in the middle of or even after the project is completed.

Starting with $20,000, this sole proprietor now heads up a $250,000 business with hopes of branching out and going beyond serving customers in her Southern California community. Her company has even attracted attention from HDTV and the DIY Network. Her success is a great example of how one can turn a passion and skill set for project management into a lucrative and much-needed business.

If you are a good manager, and love the art of coordinating teams of people, projects, and goals, ask yourself what kinds of niches that lack good management do you see in your neighborhood, city, or the world at large. Remember, you don't have to be the one to show up with all the technical know-how. Great managers often have great people skills. Great techies, on the other hand, can be weak in communication skills and may need the help of a great manager to optimize their talents and put them to good use. Imagine being at the helm of a great company that employs the best skill sets across a variety of "departments" to get a particular job done . . . and you get to call and coordinate all the main shots. Something to think about.

Dreams alone don't make money. It's the execution of dreams—ideas in action—that paves the path to millions.

COPYRIGHTS, PATENTS, AND TRADEMARKS

These three words trouble lots of people because of the common belief that these emblems of intellectual property are hard to get or cost lots of money. Not so. While going into the details of whether you should think about applying for a patent, copyright, or trademark and how to go about it is beyond the scope of this book, I do want to share that you most certainly can acquire them without breaking the bank. A patent can cost you as little as $100 to file, a trademark will cost close to $300, and a copyright rings in at a mere $45. What will cost you money, however, is hiring someone to help you decide which form of protection for your idea is best for you and then take you through the application process. Patents in particular are more difficult to apply for and can take quite a bit of time (from several months to years). The more complex the invention, the more challenging it may be to fulfill the application requirements. You don't want to burn through all your investment cash in the application process so there isn't enough left over to manufacture and launch your product into the marketplace. If this is the case, you may want to reconsider waiting to file the patent until you finish the product.

It's up to you whether you choose to finish your product before or after starting the application process. If your idea is complex and mechanical in nature, it might be a good idea to take your prototype as far as you can. Keep in mind that your prototype may require changes to avoid infringing on another patent, which is another reason to get the application going so you're ready to make those modifications.

As soon as you've fully developed your idea, determined there's a market for it, and decided to launch it, I encourage you to visit the U.S. Patent and Trademark Office at www.uspto.gov, which will give you a good starting point. For copyrights, go to the U.S. Copyright Office at www.copyright.gov.

While it isn't a good idea to jump the gun and file before fully fleshing out your idea and, shall I say, "pass Go," there is something to be said for the motivation that filing provides. Once you begin the process of obtaining legal ownership of your idea in whatever form—copyright, patent, trademark— you'll find that the energy and inspiration to make it successful will magically appear. At this level, your investment is in more than yourself.

LOCKER-ROOM STRATEGY

If you were a fly on the wall in any locker room prior to a big game, you might be surprised to hear all the encouraging and inspirational words going around in addition to actual tactical strategy. A savvy coach knows how critical attitude can be— sometimes more so than talent or skill in any given moment. Which is why any good strategy must entail a tremendous amount of attention to attitude. But how do we cultivate that perfect attitude? Is there a magic formula? Because in all honesty, it's easier said than done.

I started this chapter by telling you how you must reject the Google and Gates lie and adopt an attitude that will support you and your ideas, no matter how small you think they are. You know that I didn't go through the normal chains of educa- tion. I wasn't bogged down with thoughts of failure, and I wasn't afraid to take a few calculated risks. My positive attitude helped me stay focused and fueled from the get-go. It also helped me to ignore people who told me I couldn't do it, or that I'd be a failure soon enough. When people ask me how they, too, can nourish that same attitude and keep it moving upward, minus the ego, I share my six tips for what I call refining your character. They constitute the constant energy that you must put into enhancing yourself and maintaining a positive outlook. Some of these tips will be familiar to you because I've been hinting at them from the first chapter. It's no joke that your at- titude is your control center. I wish I could claim the phrase

"The control center of your life is your attitude," because it's just so true.

1. Faith:

Having unremitting faith in yourself and your dream is key. In the Bible, Paul said, "Faith is the substance of things hoped for and the evidence of things unseen." How can you expect anyone else to believe in your dreams or to follow your plans if you don't have faith in them yourself? Recall what I said earlier about being your own cheerleader. When you construct a plan and follow it faithfully, the universe will align itself and assist in making your dreams come true. You can call it karma or whatever you want, but any of us would be hard-pressed to name one person who succeeded without having faith in his dream.

2. Guts:

Take fear by the hand and let it lead you, even if you have to step outside your box and get a little uncomfortable. If someone tells you that she succeeded without doing anything that scared her, she is lying. Your commitment to achievement in the face of fear or what's hard is a valuable asset. Being successful means that sometimes you will have to step out of line, which means that you have to do and be things that are different from the rest of society in order to rise above *most* of society. Standing out can be scary, which is why you need guts to succeed.

Let me be clear: Having guts is different from simply not being afraid. Having guts relates to having the conviction and faith to stand strong in the pursuit of your goals no matter what others might say to distract you. Nurture an unwavering stance on the road to accomplishment and be willing to make adjustments along the way. It's perfectly natural to adjust your actions and strategies as you learn and respond to instinctual signals. Having guts will also help you make good decisions. Listen to them.

3. Determination:

Stay the course no matter what comes your way. Be solution-oriented at every step. Even if you have the guts to stay the course when times are tough, you still must possess determination to remain true to the goal. Determination means that you have resolved that no matter what life throws you, you will keep going until you reach your goal. As the old adage goes, expect to sweat it out 90 percent of the time for every 10 percent of inspiration. Issues will arise every day, some serious, some not so. Define and then prioritize the issues, coming up with techniques to maneuver around them, through them, or over them. Steadfast determination will keep your goals and vision in sight and help you seek sound solutions when you're hit by curveballs.

4. Wisdom:

Pursue the knowledge you need to achieve success in your chosen field. Again, this can entail any number of things, be it formal schooling or general life experience and personal research. Something else that can be said about successful people is that they are rarely stupid or even foolish. Keep in mind that being wise doesn't always come with age, and it is not always possessed naturally. For the most part wisdom is an understanding of what is true and right. And that understanding comes from learning, which means that anyone with determination can acquire wisdom.

I've already outlined how to do this by hunting down as much knowledge as you can about every aspect of your chosen profession. If you choose to be a real estate agent, surround yourself with other real estate agents who have been successful and who know the path you need to take to get your license. If you want to be an engineer, get acquainted with one, maybe even two or three people from different fields of engineering. Which reminds me: There are many different types of jobs within each field, so don't limit yourself to the most obvious one. Take, for example, the entertainment industry. When you think about jobs in that industry, what immediately comes to mind? Let me guess: acting, screenwriting, directing, producing. But these jobs are just the tip of the iceberg. Maybe you're not fit for a creative career, but you'd thrive on the business end because you're good with managing people and getting things done. When you know as much as you possibly can, and apply that knowledge with common sense, you will be wise enough to create your own plan for success.

Have the wisdom of patience, too. Yes, patience is still a virtue in my book, and it pays off in unexpected ways. Sometimes the answer to a problem or a possible solution won't present itself right away. This doesn't have to be a roadblock, and it doesn't mean you're in a holding pattern. It just means you are traveling on a winding section of your road, which is to be expected and can bring on new insights and lead you to your next destination. Adversity is a great teacher.

5. Focus:

Remain committed to your goal and on defining your purpose. Something that most successful people possess is the ability to excel in a variety of areas. However, because life is short and the road to success is difficult and sometimes long, you need to focus from start to finish. Focus means that you pick one activity or one area of interest and create your plan based on that one activity or area of interest. Investigate a few potential endeavors and explore the pros and cons of each one prior to making a decision, and then put your focus there. Your unique set of talents is what will bring you success, and you'll affirm your natural strengths by continually developing your inner resources.

Focus also means that when other opportunities present themselves, you weigh their value based on how they might take away your focus from the prioritized goal. Sometimes new opportunities can help you reach your initial goal, while other times they can distract you. Russell Simmons focused on music for more than ten years before branching out into fashion and comedy.

Perhaps if he had branched out sooner, his record company Def Jam would have faltered.

> Don't look for magic or luck to keep you on task toward your goal. No more hocus-pocus—stay focused!

You need to focus on your purpose. You need to focus on your goals. You need to focus on your objectives and focus on your prize. If you really want to get there, you need to focus on your target.

Also accept that failure is part of your success, and that focus will help you to stay on course when there are slip-ups. And trust me, they most certainly will happen—often when you least expect it. Dr. Roger Shank, cohost along with Maria Bartiromo of the CNBC television program *The Business of Innovation*, puts it brilliantly: "Failure is the key. You have to be failing and failing again. If we think the brilliant inventions of the world are by people who had one invention once, they had a hundred inventions, but ninety-nine of them sucked." The lesson: to be original, embrace failure. Don't let failure derail you.

This concept was made abundantly clear to me when I tried to get my teen radio gig in Vegas. From then on I learned to assume people would hand out nine no's before they offered a single yes. Some people are so negative that they *have* to say no multiple times before they can give up a positive yes. It's simply, and unfortunately, in their nature. And sometimes the rejection won't be a person or a single no. It will be an environment, economic trend, or cultural force beyond your control, as it was with my budding real estate brokerage venture that nearly went belly-up when the market closed its doors on me. I regrouped and reexamined my options to eventually discover several good yeses.

6. Integrity:

Integrity is what you do when nobody is looking. Keep a code of values and ethics that fosters greater support among your peers and family. This final component of character has been hotly debated. Some people say that it is possible to succeed without having integrity, and others say that integrity actually can get in the way when it comes to business. I say that in the short term you might win without integrity; but if you want to go far and retain the support of those around you, you have to have integrity.

Successful people who fall and fall hard often lack the code of values required to gain the support of others and prevent a fall. If you have kept your nose clean and have made certain to be fair in all of your business dealings, you will be able to worry less about people attacking you or turning their backs on you during difficult times. And most importantly, you can find more support for your goal when you have integrity. As Charles de Gaulle so eloquently put it: "Faced with crisis, the man of character falls back on himself. He imposes his own stamp of action, takes responsibility for it, and makes it his own." Also remember what I said about surrounding yourself with positivity. Avoid people who you know will bring you down and corrupt your sense of security and integrity. And separate yourself from people who no longer want to keep up their end of the bargain. You can't afford to waste your time on people who don't keep their commitment, slack off, and don't show you respect. When you are heading up a savvy and growing company, you have to be willing to let people go when they don't work out—just as you would an idea that doesn't see the light of day.

To that end, I should warn you that being an entrepreneur makes you a target for scams and thieves—people who lack a great deal of integrity but who score high on the swindling board game. Last year one of my most trusted and highly compensated employees stole from my partner and me real estate listings worth millions in a well-calculated scheme. By the time she resigned from our company she had siphoned off files in an attempt to cover up her stealing and had gotten everything primed and ready to pluck. More troubling than the financial loss was the feeling we had been defrauded on a personal level. She had befriended us, and we thought she was an honest person with integrity.

The lesson: Be careful who you trust. Be careful who you hire. As you continue to refine your character, you'll naturally become a better judge of character in others. You'll also find that the world will become an easier place and people will be more receptive to your ideas and plans. The person with character is more likely to get there than someone who is mean-spirited, lazy, or weak-hearted.

As an aside, be skeptical of any new person or group who promises to throw money at you in exchange for an "earnest money deposit." While I've never been a victim of a con artist myself, I know they are out there. Prior to accepting any money, check online fraud sites, including the Better Business Bureau (www.bbb.org) and, I repeat, trust your gut. Your gut check is a good reality check. Also check out www.LooksTooGoodToBeTrue .com, which provides a quick reference to the most common scams and how to avoid them.

THE ECONOMICS OF YOUTH

I encourage you to consider products that cater to children. The children's market is busting at the seams, and people who target the growing needs of kids stand to reap enormous financial gains. Technically kids may represent a niche market, but the amount spent by them, around them, and for them creates a terrific market opportunity too massive to ignore.

REALITY CHECK: American families spend about $115 billion a year on their children's food, clothing, personal care items, entertainment, and reading materials. Experts have projected this figure to grow to $143 billion by 2010. Coupled with the fact that the buying power of kids themselves now tops $8 billion, it doesn't pay to forget them.

Let's say your big idea happens to be a toy. You can't just walk into a toy store and start flapping your jaws to the clerk about it. Doing the knowledge will mean visiting multiple toy stores and finding out what's hot (or not). Talk to parents and kids, and consider joining organizations like the Toy Industry Association (www.toy-tia.org) to help you learn what kids want and what parents want to buy—even if you think you already know. Your next step will be to create a prototype and test its marketability. Buyers won't just want to hear about an idea—they will want to see the toy in action, to experience the fun-factor first.

The reason for this burgeoning kids market is twofold. For one, duel-income families have changed how parents find ways to juggle work and home life. And today's parents want to give every possible advantage to their children. Products and services that keep kids engaged and active, and that can potentially help them learn something new or challenging, are poised to do well. Don't underestimate the power of kids as consumers themselves, as they are logging on and navigating Web sites at an early age. It is estimated that 13.4 percent of preschoolers get information about products online.

Parents can also get ideas from their own little ones. You never know: Maybe your next big idea will come from a seven-year-old or tween. It's important to note that whether you are single or married, *you* are the single most important factor that can influence your child's growth and development. Your love and support can help put your child on the path to great success. You can teach your child the art of survival and how to solve the problems he or she will inevitably face.

You may not be able to give your children money or connections, but you can give them the values to live by: pride, respect, honest work, preparation, inspiration, the desire to give back, and the strength to never give up.

When parents ask me how they can nurture their young children so they are better prepared for the future, I give them my five top tactics:

1. Fill your home with seeds of success. Let it be a place where ideas and inspiration are welcomed and abundant. Tell your child, "You can become and do anything you set your heart and mind to." Let your child grow up believing that there are no limits to what they can do and that anything—and everything—is possible.

2. Share your words of encouragement and affirmation. Let there be plenty of "can do" conversation in your house. Eliminate any and all evidence of hopelessness from your home. Remind your children daily that they are destined for great things. When talking to your kids about career choices, stress that they should start with their interests and values. Let them know it's okay to change their minds as they learn new things and develop their skill sets. The more they are exposed to, the greater the chance they will have at finding the job that wins their heart. They shouldn't feel rushed or grim about their future. Life is too short not to approach your career and future with a genuine sense of adventure.

3. Show your kids the values of dedicated work and open-hearted love. Get them up with a kiss as you leave for work. Kiss them as you come home after a hard day. No matter how much money you have or don't have, be a culinary and financial genius and a super parent—and show them how to turn a bag of potatoes, a can of beans, a package of ground beef, and a loaf of bread into delicious meals that last all week. Put tender loving care into the small things you do no matter how scarce the resources are.

4. Engender and encourage independence and an attitude of self-reliance. Take your kids to an all-you-can-eat restaurant and have them bring their own plastic containers and plastic bags to take home leftovers. Drive home the lesson that "you always want to have a backup plan." Teach them that no one's going to change it, so what's the point of complaining?

5. Encourage your children to work and make money. Believe in them and help them taste the sweet smell of success. Teach your children to get away from the lottery ticket mentality and work to make money to support hobbies and the purchase of personal items. Let them start businesses, work for neighbors, babysit, or mow lawns. Encourage them to be creative and make things to sell. Let them experience the thrill of creating something themselves and selling it. This experience will help them recognize their passions, talents, and purpose in life. Only then may they discover their true selves and find work they love.

Help your kids find good mentors and teachers early on. There are always good people around to help you raise your child. Just keep looking for them until you find them. Don't give up asking for help. That's not begging—it's investing in your child's future. There are a lot of good people in this world. Find them and put your children near them.

Remember, great careers and successful lives start with small ideas and baby steps. Give yourself permission to let your child experiment. Keep your eyes and mind open and be ready to work with your children. Adults don't always hit home runs on the first or second or third try, and children don't, either. But they'll never hit a home run if they don't learn to swing. Your child may make only five dollars on her first business.

But it will probably be the most important five dollars she ever makes.

INVENTION AND INTENTIONS ARE NOT ENOUGH

Sorry to be the bearer of bad news, but this shouldn't come as a surprise: Brilliant inventions and good intentions are not enough to make you rich. The missing word? Come on, you should know this by now: ACTION. There may be no better way to take that initial action, especially if you are unsure of what to do, than to sit down and hammer out a business plan. Remember the missions and goals I talked about in Chapter 5? Well, there's no better way to attach action to your missions and goals than to map it all out in a business plan. Whether you go to the moon and back in crafting your written business plan or just jot down a rough cut of a plan, I'm a big believer in them. This goes for people who aim to approach investors formally or just flesh out ideas with a future "start date" in mind. That start date can be the day you begin to transition step by step from your current job to becoming self-employed or the day you actually leave your current job and establish your own business.

Very few small-business owners engage in formal business planning. Rarely do they invest the time to examine their business goals and create the best means for accomplishing them. As an aspiring start-up entrepreneur you may wonder why it's so important to prepare a written plan. You may believe that it will require too much time—time you think would be more profitably invested in actual business operations. I'll be honest, planning does require a considerable time investment, but the time spent in planning is recovered many times over in increased efficiency and an improved product or service. The planning process forces you to take an objective and critical view of the project in its entirely.

Business plans can work wonders for you. They are part road map, part marketing tool—guiding your business management but also providing the means to communicate your ideas to those who may be considering investing in your business, be it friends or general investors. There are a number of good software programs available to help you craft and format your plan. I've got some leads on my own site that you can check out, too. The added virtue of making a business plan is that it helps you to understand the various aspects of business operations and how they relate to each other. The plan will lead you through the process of exploring your competition, gaining a keen sense of your market, identifying your customers, and turning your idea into money. You'll develop realistic goals and procedures to implement the strategies outlined in each functional area of the plan.

To that end, let me share my Great 8 Start-up Essentials:

1. An idea:

It should be fleshed out because you've done the knowledge and have identified a potential market.

2. A business plan:

Take this seriously, even if you don't complete a model plan worthy of publication, and even if you don't plan to raise capital outside your personal savings and access to funds. You'll need a business plan to clarify the vision you have for your idea, as well as for yourself.

3. Bookkeeping and accounting basics:

Because you'll likely have to wear a few hats in the first days of your business, you'll have to get comfortable with some basic math to keep track of the finances of your business. Don't get intimidated by this. Again, there are lots of resources *for free* on the Internet to help you learn about things like breakeven analysis and other common business accounting terms to get you up to speed.

4. Me, myself, and I:

Few businesses start out with a full staff. You will add people to your core workforce (which at the start may be just you) as you can afford them and as you require new sets of skills mastered by others. It's important that when you do hire others that you find highly motivated people who enjoy the dynamics of working for a small start-up business and who can perform their jobs well. Student interns with specific areas of specialization and work experience can be of great, inexpensive help.

5. Time management:

This is another one of those easier-said-than-done tips. Some of us are better at managing our time than others. Regardless of which category you come under, it helps to chart out your tasks and check off your to-dos on a daily, weekly, and monthly basis. Keep both a planning and an operations log. These tools will help you avoid oversights and provide vital information when memory fails. For example, set aside the same time every day to visit your operations log and assess what you've gotten done for the day and what still needs to be accomplished. Get into a routine of keeping your to-dos in check. Plan on having an extra fifteen to twenty minutes at the end of the day to take care of unfinished business or a task that has taken longer than expected.

6. Legal matters:

The entrepreneur has to be well-versed in local and state government rules and regulations governing small businesses. This entails choosing the most appropriate legal form of doing business, such as becoming incorporated and fulfilling those requirements and filing tax returns—both personal and business. This all may sound complicated, but it really isn't. Getting incorporated, for instance, is as easy as filling out a few forms and filing them with the appropriate government entity and paying a fee. You can do this with a legal document company or by asking an accountant to help you out. Once you have your business incorporated, you can then set up a bank account in its name and begin to conduct business from the account. For more help in understanding your particular state's rules, plus help in accessing resources tailored to your state's specific business regulations, I recommend visiting your state's main Web site (try www .yourstate.gov). If you live in a major metropolitan area, you may also find it helpful to visit your city's main Web site. Or choose the nearest city by you and see if they offer information for business owners online. You may, for instance, have to obtain a business license even if you are starting a small operation from home. These are usually inexpensive and you can qualify for exemption in your beginning years.

7. Clients and customers:

These golden gems usually begin knocking on your door once you have done some savvy marketing and advertising. But don't mistake savvy for spendy. Plenty of marketing strategies come on the cheap these days through the Internet and old-fashioned methods of advertising (think flyers, word of mouth, community events, and the Yellow Pages). Promote your business through a Web site, which you can build yourself using any of the packages that typically come with setting up a domain name. When you establish an account at Yahoo! Business, for example, you can get a free downloadable software program that guides you step by step through creating a Web site using your chosen domain name. You also can set up e-mail accounts and access a host of digital tools to build your site. If at all possible, try to integrate content on your site so you can generate online commerce. Your site can be minimal at first, but as you grow you'll want to consider improving your layout and design to give your site a competitive edge.

8. Support system:

Okay, so when you start a business you are filled with excitement and energy. Most likely you're also experiencing some anxiety, fear, worry, trepidation, hesitation, dread, panic, terror . . . need I continue? This is why it's critical to have a strong support system on hand so you can talk out your biggest fears and keep your confidence level high. Most family members and friends can play this role, but be careful. Some may want to sabotage you. Some may fear your success and do whatever they can to derail you. Work on growing your support system, weeding out the toxic people when necessary, and keeping up your affirmations. When I was faced with a serious decision recently, someone said to me, "Be your authentic self." That cleared the air up instantly. It's now an affirmation I use to remind myself that I've got what it takes to succeed if I just listen to myself, stay positive, and go with my gut. Recall how I said earlier that it's unrealistic to think you won't encounter unfamiliar territory for which you will need to seek some outside help. Developing a circle of associates for this very purpose is key. You can all help each other find new, innovative ways of resolving problems. You'll be surprised by what else you can get out of this. The exchange of information will further support your enthusiasm, strengthen new talents, and reinforce your determination to succeed.

After Jared Diamond wrote the bestselling *Guns, Germs, and Steel,* which was first published in 1999 and won him the Pulitzer Prize, he came out with another book called *Collapse: How Societies Choose to Fail or Succeed.* In *Guns, Germs, and Steel,* Diamond explains the geographic and environmental reasons why some human populations have flourished, and in *Collapse* he uses the same factors to examine why ancient societies have fallen apart, especially the most famed civilizations in prehistory and modern history, like the Anasazi of the American Southwest, Easter Islanders, and the Viking colonies of Greenland. He also touches on modern ones, such as Rwanda. Both books are powerful—part riveting, part unsettling; they bring to light many ideas on how societies can routinely fall prey to environmental and economic disasters, as well as a profound inability to respond to and prepare for an imminent disaster. I love how Diamond uses the verb "choose." By saying societies *choose* to either fail or succeed, it places responsibility on them. And it's true that we either choose to fail or succeed in life—there's no one else to blame for our failures but ourselves.

It's amazing to me how one can foresee a disaster and do nothing about it. But then I remind myself: This happens all the time in business, and especially with entrepreneurs.

I'm not alone in this thinking. Business writer Keith McFarland has written on this exact topic. In 2005 he wrote an article for *BusinessWeek* that compared Diamond's message and theme in *Collapse* to start-ups. And I couldn't agree with him more. According to McFarland, start-ups fail for the same reasons societies fail. When times get tough, mistakes get made. In particular, McFarland points out four common mistakes that happen: 1) a failure to anticipate problems; 2) a failure to respond promptly when problems occur; 3) an inability to behave rationally; and 4) an adoption of so-called "disastrous values."

These first two reasons should be self-explanatory. Behaving irrationally can be any number of things that just won't help you get out of a fix. For example, cutting costs by firing the one person who brings in the most sales would be considered irrational. An example of adopting "disastrous values" would be to hold on to old ways of thinking (i.e., that the CEO is always right) and not let your team of people strategize for themselves and, as McFarland points out, "contribute meaningfully to [the company's] strategy." A company (and, let's not forget, a society) must continue to evolve and adapt to its own growth. What works in the beginning stages of development may not be as effective as—and may, in fact, undermine—later stages.

It's natural as an entrepreneur to be optimistic. We don't want to think about potential problems, much less plan for them. We may be able to figure a way out of a particularly hairy problem, but what happens when we hit a really big problem? This is what separates those who succeed and those who are forced to call it quits when a crisis of monumental size emerges and you don't have enough water on hand to douse the flames.

The good news (and the lesson to take away here) is that we can choose how to think. We can *choose* whether or not we decide to pay attention to upcoming problems. We can *choose* to listen to catalysts, signals, signs, and so on. And we can *choose* to deal with problems as quickly as possible when they emerge. In the next chapter I'll be giving you my final tips to problem solving, but right now I want you to understand that your success will rely on the choices you make. That's it. All that I've been telling you up to now reiterates this pure and simple truth. Which also goes back to why I insist on planning. Like the old saying goes: If you fail to plan, you plan to fail.

Challenges come so we can grow and be prepared for things we are not equipped to handle now. When we face our challenges with faith, prepared to learn, willing to make changes, and if necessary, to let go, we are demanding our power be turned on.

— IYANLA VANZANT

7

The Wall Street Lie

Lie: I have to know a lot about the stock market or work on the Street to be rich.

Truth: Returns on investments don't come directly from Wall Street. They arise from within you based on what you know and love.

A picture doesn't always tell a story—particularly one about wealth. When you watch someone pull up to the curb in a luxury vehicle and step out wearing designer clothing and a platinum watch, you automatically think, "Wow, that person must be rich." It's human to pass judgment and be fooled by outer appearance. Yes, *fooled*. You'd be surprised by how many well-dressed and accessorized people carry enormous amounts of consumer debt and have nothing to speak for in terms of assets that *increase* in value over time, such as real estate and stocks. Warren Buffett, one of the richest individuals in the world, is famous for his frugal and unpretentious lifestyle. He still lives in the same house he bought in Omaha, Nebraska, for $31,500 in 1958. He does not carry a cell phone, does not have a computer at his desk, frequently dines at Dairy Queen, and drives his own car (a Cadillac GTS).

That said, one of biggest misconceptions is that the only way to be rich is to invest on Wall Street or in real estate. We hear about "rich" people with multiple homes and their own private stockbrokers or "asset managers" on Wall Street. These two types of investments weigh heavily on many people's minds, especially if they feel they're not adequate, smart, or rich enough to participate in the Wall Street or real estate game. Let me tell you otherwise.

The truth behind the Wall Street lie is pretty straightforward and simple: Investments don't live on Wall Street. They live in you—in what you know. You can make money collecting vintage Coke bottles and you can make money buying Coke stock. You can make money buying toys and dolls, or you can buy stock in the company that sells those products. You can make money buying real estate, and you can make money buying real estate investment trusts (aka REITS on Wall Street). You can make money investing in a business, or you can make money buying businesses in the form of stock on Wall Street. It doesn't make a difference. The truth of the matter is when you invest in what you know (and I assume like), you stand to gain a healthy return over time as you watch that investment grow in value.

The Wall Street Truth: Returns on investments don't come directly from Wall Street. They arise from within you based on what you know and love.

PUT A WINDOW IN THE WALL: INVEST IN WHAT YOU KNOW

Wall Street has always carried an aura of prestige, wealth, and status. It exudes that old-boys'-club feeling. Even the word *wall* is fitting—it seems more like a wall few can penetrate than a street anyone can walk down. Indeed, much of the financial world revolves around Wall Street and the transactions that take place on the stock exchanges. But focusing too much on "the Street" is a waste of time and energy for those looking to be successful. The Street has nothing to do with achievement. At least not in the way conventional wisdom dictates.

I challenge you to put a window on Wall Street—to look inside at what's really going on: People are investing in what they know and love. Most people who trade on Wall Street have a passion for following the stocks of certain companies and they often invest in businesses that they know very well. But anyone can do this on any level, not just with pieces of paper on a formal trading floor.

People have become collectors and investors in items as cheap as baseball cards, coins, cars, furniture, gemstones, paintings, comic books, antiques, Beanie Babies, Barbie action figures, dollhouses, and so on. I have a friend who has collected dolls for years and who now boasts a collection worth six figures. A quick tour of eBay or any online auction site shows you just what can fetch a fine dollar. In fact, I bet that the value of many homespun investments rivals the investments we see on Wall Street or in real estate.

REALITY CHECK: The same logic that a Wall Street investor would apply to buying stocks is the same logic anyone would employ to invest in anything of potential future value. For example, when you buy a home, you do some homework first. You consider how much it will cost you, how much you can afford, the condition of the house, and so on. When you buy a car, you do enough homework so you know you are getting a good deal (well, at least most of us do this). Granted, cars don't typically appreciate over time, but you do want to be sure it has a high resale value. If you're an aficionado of Civil War paraphernalia, when you come across a new item to add to your collection, be sure it's authentic and worth the amount you're going to pay today. Don't buy on impulse without doing your homework. The word *invest* does come with instructions: Take your time before purchasing. It wouldn't be an investment if it didn't bear extra weight.

When deciding whether to buy common, everyday items, we all pretty much experience a similar thought pattern. We do our research and then go with our gut. It's common sense. And once you've done enough research to satisfy yourself, you know a heck of a lot more than if you had made your purchase based only on what you heard or what your best friend told you. At the end of the day, you have to trust your instinct, and since all investments are risky to some degree, you know how much easier it is to feel comfortable taking the plunge with an investment you know— and know very well.

So let's go back to Wall Street and see if we can't knock a

window or two out of it. I want you to begin to see the word *investment* as something that starts with you, something that may have nothing to do with the Street per se. When you invest in yourself and honor those things that you know and love, you can reap big rewards that will enrich your future.

EXACTLY WHAT SHOULD I INVEST IN?

I get this question from a lot of people, and I know they are looking for an answer beyond the "what you know" mantra. I do, however, encourage them to consider first what they understand and have a general interest in, and then to move forward from there. But some want specifics on investments that are guaranteed to create a profit, regardless of how familiar they are with the investment. Don't expect me to give you any particulars—if I tell you to buy gold or oil, guess what?: By the time you read this, they may be bad investments. But I will say this: Invest, don't save. Now that may sound contrary to common sense, but soon you'll know exactly what I mean.

INVEST, DON'T SAVE

Recall my recommendations about savings in Chapter 5. Your net worth is the difference between your assets (what you *own*) and your liabilities (what you *owe*). If you have more assets than liabilities, congratulations: You are in the positive. In addition to socking away whatever you can each month based on your payments toward debts (and other lie-abilities), I want you to come up with more powerful ways to watch those savings increase your net worth. And when I say "invest, don't save," what I mean is you should start looking for financial vehicles that will store or utilize your savings *and* pay interest on them or allow you to realize an appreciation of some sort. Examples span the gamut, from high-interest savings accounts, bonds, and certificates of deposit to stocks, mutual funds, foreign currencies, precious metals, real estate, and others. In other words, don't stash cold hard cash under your mattress, in a closet, or in your momma's jewelry box. Get real with real money: Make it make money!

First, understand the power of compound growth; it's the most important financial tool you can use and was named the eighth wonder of the world by Warren Buffett. In short, it's how money makes money. Translation: free money. It's like putting two rabbits in a room and coming back to find that they have multiplied to twenty. The longer you stay out of the room, the more rabbits you get. Let me put this into perspective.

Say you're thirty years old. You want to have a million dollars by the age of sixty-five. You've got thirty-five years to make it, or 420 months to reach that goal. One million divided by 420 equals $2,381 per month to save. But this is without counting the time value of money. Not many of us can save that much a month and keep it locked up. That's why we need to employ the magic of compound *interest* to get to our goal line faster. You see, money not only earns interest, but interest earns interest. Instead of feeding the piggy bank endlessly (i.e., money), you invest your money at a certain rate (i.e., allowing it to accrue interest) for a predetermined time. Example: You invest $1,000 and it gets an annual return of 10 percent. After the first year, your investment is worth $1,100, so now you have more money to invest and generate an even greater return. In the second year, you get a return of 10 percent on that $100 profit *as well as* your original $1,000. This brings your total to $1,210, and so on. This keeps going, so if you leave your investment to compound at 10 percent per year, fifty years later that $1,000 becomes $117,391—without you doing *anything*. Now imagine how much faster and greater that sum would increase if, in addition to letting it grow based on interest payments alone, you continue to add more money to the baseline, the principal. If you save just $25 a week for forty years, even with just half of that return—a measly 5 percent—you will have more than $165,000.

That, my friends, is the power of compound growth. Ten percent can make a lot of money in the long term. So can 5 percent, which is what a high-yielding savings account may offer; or 7 percent, which is a very conservative number for the average returns in the stock market (historically stock market returns average 10 percent each year); or 15 to 20 percent, which is what some savvy stock traders do when they learn the ropes on Wall Street and follow the trading trends. Time is perhaps the most critical ingredient here; the more you have of it, the less money you need to reach your goal. At 10 percent, a twenty-year-old only needs to sock away $135 per month or $4.50 per day to become a millionaire by sixty-five. If you wait until you're forty years old, you'll need to put away $892 per month or almost $30 per day to reach the same goal.

I confess, I'm not about to discuss the present or future value of money or the time value of money. It's a subject worthy of a separate book itself. For starters, go to www.kiplinger.com or www.smartmoney.com for calculators to help you plug in the numbers to arrive at how many years it will take to make $X at X percent interest given how much you invest. It's a simple equation that takes into consideration the investment dollar amount, the amount of time you have, and the interest rate paid; the calculators will do all the math for you. From there you can then shop around for the right investment vehicle to bring you to your goal. Each one will bear its own risks and potential rewards.

Many investments have added benefits like tax deductions or protective shields to avoid paying capital gains taxes, which are what we owe the government when we take profits from our investments. Uncle Sam always likes to gets paid when there's a profit made, even if he hasn't done anything to generate that profit. But now there are a few financial vehicles that can limit the amount of money you have to dole out to Uncle Sam for your hard investment work. This is especially true for vehicles like Roth IRAs (IRA is short for investment retirement account; there are a few varieties of IRAs). If you work for a company that offers 401(k) or 403(b) plans, which allow you to save and receive a tax deduction, do what you can to contribute to those plans. If your company matches a portion of your investment, they are as close to free money as you can get. As you receive raises you can designate a higher portion of your income to increase your savings. With online banking, it is now easy to learn a lot about different types of investment accounts without having to meet face to face with an advisor or visit your bank. Check out sites like www.fool.com and www.money.cnn.com. They are great starting points for learning more about how to make money work for you.

Bonds are other financial entities to consider when you've got enough to set aside. Bonds represent loans to the government or corporate entities, and they typically pay you interest twice a year. Commodities, including raw materials like oil, natural gas, gold, silver, coffee, fruit, grains, and meats, are another option. When inflation rises, our purchasing power is reduced, and this causes stocks and bonds to fall. But commodities and real estate prices will often increase. Having a good sense of the business and economic cycles throughout the year in relation to the stock market is key. But don't panic. You don't need to enroll in a heavy-duty Econ class to get this knowledge. You would be amazed at what you can find if you put the time in to read. Lots of established business writers cover these and many other related topics in engaging, fun-to-read articles and blogs online. You just have to find the ones you enjoy reading—and take some notes. In fact, there are so many online business writers these days you can find a financial expert who shares your interests, age, and general lifestyle (you'll know it when you find writing that can "speak" to you—it's not like trying to swallow a tedious teacher's lessons). Just make sure you know you are getting sound advice and information from a legit, well-known site. This won't guarantee that you won't ever come across questionable information—especially in a field as speculative as forecasting economic climates—but it's the best you can do.

Speaking of the Internet and access to resources, it's never been easier to get educated in the stock market and keep a trading account now that there are low-cost brokers like Scottrade, Ameritrade, Sharebuilder.com, and eTrade. I know that for many this still may seem like a scary wall to climb, but I encourage you to investigate stocks that relate to your passion and interest. If you drink Coke every day and love to download music on iTunes, maybe Coke in the form of KO and Apple in the form of AAPL would be great stock picks for you to research and follow. (KO is the ticker symbol for Coke, and AAPL is the symbol for Apple, which is traded on the NASDAQ.) If you did buy into those funky Croc shoes and they line your closet, you weren't the only one helping its stock skyrocket. Croc has experienced a meteoric rise in price nearly unprecedented in modern footwear stocks. Also remember that you're not investing on Wall Street per se *even when you buy a stock*. You are investing in what you know and love.

The number of online sites dedicated to helping you become a smart stock trader and understand how Wall Street works is truly remarkable. In just the last five years alone there has been an enormous migration of financial research tools to the Internet that previously had been hoarded by professionals. Now many of them are free for people like you and me so we can become our own professionals. It just takes time and a little effort to get acquainted with these tools and the market. A few to get you started: www.seekingalpha.com, http://moneycentral.msn.com, www.morningstar.com, http://finance.yahoo.com, and http://finance.google.com. You don't need a big investment to get going—start with whatever you can spare. Turn on CNBC once in a while and tune into the goings-on.

Here's another idea to help you extend your network: Start an investment club. Gather together a group of friends or family members and pool your money to invest as a group in the market. This adds to the fun factor and forces an exchange of ideas and thoughts on companies that potentially can enhance your trading skills and knowledge. The National Association of Investors Corporation (www.betterinvesting.org) has all the information you need to get your investment club in gear. The Internet also has resources (try any of the above sites).

As a last-ditch resort, if single stocks aren't for you and you just can't invest the time to research and follow your favorite companies, then consider mutual funds. Mutual funds are groups of stocks—your money is pooled with other people's money and managed by a fund manager. You get to choose the mutual fund, but you don't get to choose the individual stocks (and sometimes bonds) that make up that fund. When you invest in a mutual fund, you are buying shares (or portions) of the mutual fund and you become a shareholder of the fund. There are thousands to choose from, and you can find them at any online trading site. Brokerage-firm representatives can also help you navigate your way around mutual funds.

GET REAL WITH REAL ESTATE

This is an important step, whether you are currently a home-owner or not. I'm a huge believer in the power of owning real estate. In fact, I don't just own personal and income properties—by now you also know I own real estate companies that further increase my net worth exponentially each and every year. The evidence in favor of real estate is compelling. A report put out by the National Association of Realtors in early 2007, which as you'll recall was during a time when the real estate market had begun to soften considerably, said that typical sellers were still experiencing healthy gains on the value of their homes over the previous five years, including areas where prices had fallen. The median five-year price gain was 41.8 percent. In general, real estate doesn't have the volatility that the stock market has, and if there's one thing owning property can offer above other types of investments, it's leverage, which can more than triple your returns in real estate, even while the income easily pays down the principal.

What's more, according to wealth strategist Michael Masterson, the average person with a net worth of $6.8 million owns a primary residence worth $545,000. How is this possible? Because owning even a relatively inexpensive home accelerates wealth building. It lowers your taxes and the money you plow into the home—paying for utilities, maintenance, upgrades, furnishings, and so on essentially adds to its capacity to appreciate in value, while also doubling as a nice place to live and raise a family. After all, we all have to live somewhere. Might as well own the place where you live and gain the rewards that come with that ownership. And get this: If you were to manipulate Masterson's statistic, then you could reach a net worth of $1 million with an $80,000 house. That's certainly something to think about.

But real estate comes with a few caveats. You must prepare yourself for taking on the responsibilities that accompany being a property owner, and you must maintain that responsibly once you're a member of that club. If you find yourself locked in an interest-only loan, you may as well call yourself a renter. You are renting from the bank, which is sucking money from you and leaving you equity dry. In the past ten years financial institutions have gone wild, offering too-good-to-be-true mortgages that allow you to "creatively finance" a piece of property. Government officials are now pushing for new legislation to help put an end to predatory lending practices. At this writing, mortgage delinquencies and foreclosures are on the rise, as many are falling prey to the whims of their adjustable-rate mortgages. As soon as those monthly payments creep up, some of which can explode in a blink, you could be left wondering what happened to your initial deal. And you may be on the losing side of the game, with no leverage and no way out unless you sell at a loss.

Take, for example, a $300,000 house that you buy with an interest-only loan. Two years later the market has downshifted and now your abode is worth $250,000—$50,000 less than what you paid. Now, if you're in it for the long haul, you can wait out this (hopefully) temporary downturn in the market and see your house increase in value again. But what if other events in your life don't go as planned? What if, as in the case of my friend Shanel, you begin to get low on funds and you need to access money for purposes of pursuing other goals or, in a worst-case scenario, just to keep up with your basic living expenses? You can't cash out equity in your home because you don't have any. You can't even sell it because you can't pay the bank. To do so, you must come up with that $50,000 gap plus a real estate agent's commission (6 percent), plus all the fees related to the transaction. So if you do sell it at a loss, you're in further debt, which weakens your opportunities to pursue other goals.

So you can see how I'm not a cheering supporter of those fancy loopholes financial institutions make to get people to sign on the dotted line today and beg for a reversal of fortune later on. For most Americans, owning a home ranks number one on their list of dreams to realize. It's often touted as the clearest, easiest, and single best pathway to wealth, which is true when you look at the larger picture and consider its potential to reap incredible gains and, for all intents and purposes, perpetuate its own compound growth through serial real estate deals.

But here's the problem: Many people tend to believe that owning real estate creates sudden and sustainable wealth, and as such should be a top priority at all costs. After all, home ownership automatically provides leverage for other financial goals, such as financing a child's education, paying down debt, and funding a business. Right? Well, as many of you have noticed from stories in the media in the past year, this isn't always the case. Millions of Americans are now struggling to stay afloat with their mortgage payments and other bills, and their homes are incredibly large inconveniences that are slowly leading to total paralysis. They are stuck in the quicksand of an acute short-term crisis and can't wait for help to arrive in the long term. And when it comes to real estate, long-term thinking is, for the most part, a secret.

Home ownership should be a goal on everyone's radar, but it should be achieved when the time is right. You'll know it's right when you can avoid no-money-down mortgage offers, put at least 10 percent down initially, and not feel shackled to your mortgage payment each month. I'd rather see you build your savings and fund a 401(k) or IRA long before you set your sights on getting into real estate. In the meantime, surround yourself with sound knowledge and news about the real estate market. Become familiar with the ins and outs of buying and selling, whether for personal reasons like owning a home or for investment purposes, as in an income property. Real estate is an industry in itself, complete with seminars, books, and home-study programs. You must do the knowledge in this arena as you would if you were starting a business. If you're not well-versed in real estate, you're either not ready to invest or you're not trying hard enough to fully prepare yourself. Studying up before taking the plunge will help you navigate all your options in light of your personal goals. You'll learn, for example, that 100 percent financing actually *can* be a great opportunity for investors buying income properties such as an apartment building or medical building with tenants. It's just not a strategy for people seeking a home to live in.

I also recommend getting some counseling prior to the

mortgage plunge. According to a study that analyzed 40,000 mortgages originated under Freddie Mac's Affordable Gold program, the group of borrowers who received individual counseling had a 34 percent lower delinquency rate than those who didn't. Where can you find a housing counselor? Most work for nonprofit organizations, such as NeighborWorks (www.nw.org) and ACORN Housing (www.acornhousing.org), although some lenders and insurers also keep counselors on staff. To find a local home-buying program in your area, go the HUD Web site (www .hud.gov) and click on your state for a listing of all the agencies it funds. You also could try contacting your state or county housing finance agency. Many church groups, credit unions, and employers also have relationships with local counselors.

When there is a housing slowdown, you'll want to consider foreclosures and government repos. Also think about FSBOs—For Sale by Owner, which typically are good deals for buyers. It helps to work with a savvy real estate agent who is knowledgeable about the area where you want to live. You can work with an agent and still buy an FSBO house. Share your home-buying dreams with everyone you know to naturally expand your househunting eyes. You'd be surprised how much advice and information you can gather through your own networks once you put the word out. You'll also get help in locating good deals and perhaps considering neighborhoods you may not have had on your list.

For those already saddled with a mortgage that isn't doing much for you (and you know who you are), I say it's time to reevaluate. I can't tell you whether to sell or hold; that's a decision you'll have to determine on your own. It may help to speak with a financial wizard who can evaluate your current circumstances in light of your future financial goals and guide you in the right direction. Each person's situation will be different. My message to you is clear: Keep real estate on your list of goals, but learn how to swim before diving in. Position yourself to enter the real estate market with a splash, trained to ride any potentially rough currents, and you will come out a winner.

INVEST IN YOUR OWN BUSINESS

You know I'm not going to let you go on this one. I've been giving you a lot of information about where to put your money and how to start thinking like a bona fide investor. But here's a harsh reality: It's very difficult to make millions at a regular 9 to 5 job with modest increases in income while investing your money on the side in an interest-bearing account or through other financial vehicles. The old-fashioned pinch, save, and wait approach won't get you to millions in a short time period. It's similar to the problem that serious debt can cause—it can be very difficult if not impossible to get out of deep debt while working with a fixed income. You must find new ways to tap greater sources of income to clean up your financial house quickly. You must "un-fix" your income.

In the examples above we saw how it could take decades to reach a million. Yes, compound interest is amazing, but it won't win on the racetrack against someone who's got premium fuel in the tank thanks to the blessings of a high, unfixed income. You're constantly at the mercy of how much you have to invest, how long you have to invest, and your rate of return. You are also at the mercy of inflation and taxes, both of which can ruthlessly filch your hard-earned dollars. How much you have to invest is more in your control than rates of return and time. And that, clearly, relates directly to income.

REALITY CHECK: Unless you can substantially increase your income or, in a perfect world, break free from a fixed income, you won't get rich in the near future.

So how do you increase your income? Well, you'll recall in Chapter 4 my strategies for increasing income, such as getting more aggressive about raises, taking on a larger role in your company, creating passive streams of income, and thinking about starting your own business where the sky is the limit on potential earnings. Truth be told, the vast majority of millionaires and billionaires got rich through the various businesses they started or helped run. Did you get that? I also said *helped run*. As I've been telling you throughout the book, not everyone may aspire to be a full-fledged entrepreneur, and I respect that. That doesn't mean you can't become the next-best-thing to owning a wonderful company that makes a lot of money: being its most indispensable employee or leader.

If you become an invaluable member of an organization, no matter how big or small, you will no doubt welcome numerous financial benefits that can translate to millions. Top positions at many companies can offer equity in the company, which, as a stakeholder, means you are entitled to a percentage of the profits. Top positions also call for higher salaries, thicker bonuses, and better benefits in general. You even may find yourself sitting in the office of CEO someday. It may not have been the company you founded, got going, and saw through all the tough times. But now it's the company you've helped run of late, and you've become a priceless member by helping it continue to grow, increase revenues, and transform itself through the years. This is exactly what Jack Welch did to GE, what Darwin Smith did for the old paper company Kimberly-Clark, and what Ursula Burns is doing now for Xerox. In fact, any of the model Level 5 leaders that Jim Collins chronicles in his astounding book *Good to Great* qualify. If you can help a company go from "good to great," you will find *yourself* going from good to great as well.

Okay, so you may be thinking, If I want to start a business, does that count as an investment? And how do you juggle paying down debt, setting up investment accounts with hard-to-find savings, yada, yada, yada? Is this realistic?

Of course it is. I don't expect you to get rich overnight. Aim to have a combination of investments, including stocks, real estate, CDs, bonds, and businesses—whether they be solely your own or a piece of a larger organization. You also can consider investing in other people's businesses. Just be sure to do your homework, even if it's your Curious George cousin or brother with a self-proclaimed brilliant idea.

Any business you sink money into is an investment, even if it's your own. Because start-ups typically require you to invest your own dollars and personal funds to get started, you'll find the priorities figuring themselves out. You won't be buying a home or heavily investing in stocks and bonds, for instance, if your money is tied up in the beginning stages of your business. If you already own a home and a few investment accounts, then I recommend speaking with a financial advisor about the possibility of tapping those sources for the purposes of fueling your fledgling business. These can be a source of extra start-up money when used wisely. But each person's individual situation will be different, which is why I can't give any blanket recommendation here. Again, I repeat: Nothing happens overnight. Be patient with yourself. You may not be able to predict the fortieth step you'll take from today, but by the time you reach the thirty-ninth step you'll know what to do to move forward smartly. Keep in mind that not all businesses last forever. You may, for example, have so much success in your little venture that you'll find bigger companies offering to buy you out—usually for large amounts of money. That may be how one of your stories ends, but guess what: You get to take that money and start another business. How much fun is that?

Serial success by "serial-preneurs" is becoming the norm in today's world. Conventional wisdom may say that most entrepreneurs struggle their whole lives to bring one idea or thing to market. Reality Check: This "wisdom" is now myth. There's a rapidly growing breed of entrepreneurs who have hits one after the other. Their secret? Well, according to a study that Professor Wayne Stewart of Clemson University published in 2000 with two other researchers, it boils down to the same characteristics

I've been talking about: passion, drive, ambition, hustle. Serial-preneurs love the thrill of starting a new business. They bring honed skills from one business to the other, as well as their support systems, networks, and connections that they've built. They also bring two other very important assets to future rounds: experience and credibility. They view money as the means to an end—and not the end! Which explains why someone would take a $10 million cash-out in a business venture and roll it into a new business rather than a bank account on which to "retire." In fact, young entrepreneurs who hit it big often report *trying* to retire on their wealth but ending up back in the game because retirement makes them depressed, insecure, incredibly bored, and unhappy.

Speaking of youth, don't forget that there's no such thing as being "too young" to start a business. Teens who make it big in biz now have a name: High School Moguls. That's what Mark J. Penn called them in his recent book *Microtrends*, where he explains the burst in teen entrepreneurship in recent years with the help of the Internet. The majority of teens (more than seven in ten) admit to wanting to be their own boss someday. That's good news to hear—especially since getting a "teen mogul" label, which was what I got, can make you feel isolated. I bet the High School Mogul community will only get larger. They will increasingly be a driving force in the economy.

Driving Up Millions from the Inner City

For Dawson Rutter, founder and president of a top-tier limousine service company called Commonwealth Worldwide, getting into a taxi brings him feelings of immense nostalgia. It was behind the wheel of a cab that a lightbulb shined brightly over his head, illuminating his path to creating one of the most trusted professional limo services, catering to financial executives, entertainers, and other VIPs. A serial college dropout with a penchant for taking on any oddball job that came his way, Rutter gained most of his knowledge and business savvy from life. Drifting from jobs such as a construction worker, waiter, short-order cook, lawn mower, auto mechanic, and sheet-metal worker, Rutter may not have foreseen his rich future the day he decided to transport businesspeople and lumbering drunks alike through the streets of Boston. Life as a taxi driver taught him many things, but one lesson he learned quite well from the get-go was how the quality of customer service could make or break a business. He also had a keen awareness of the dearth of quality care in his industry, and he knew his line of work could benefit from greater attention to details (picture well-tailored chauffeurs with polished shoes) to be able to provide supreme service. In fact, some say Rutter's experience as an employee at poorly run companies put a big chip on his shoulder, making him obsessed with good customer service.

But today high-quality service is his claim to fame—it's his area of excellence, and through the years it has earned him more than kudos from loyal clients, including celebrities. Now reportedly worth $34 million, Rutter's company is setting its own benchmarks and proving that minor details like polished shoes and looking people in the eye to judge whether a firm handshake is appropriate do matter. Rutter has been written about a lot in the past year, as he is setting new standards of success as one of the country's fastest-growing inner-city start-up companies.

Rutter's story shares many of the same characteristics of many other success stories. He has blended together knowledge, experience, drive, hustle, and ambition. He combined his knack for making good decisions with his zeal for putting the customer first. He acquired much of his knowledge through the ten years he spent driving and dispatching taxis before a friend lured him over to the limo business. It was an offer impossible to pass up. As a chauffeur he'd get to drive an air-conditioned car, which was especially appealing during the hot and humid Boston summer months. He knew he'd also avoid some of those riff-raff clients he'd encountered in the ordinary cab business. Rutter grabbed on to every opportunity to advance in the company, and when an operations manager left for vacation just one month after he had arrived on the scene, he enthusiastically filled the temporary vacancy. He proved he could do the job exceptionally well, and it soon became his full-time position. Nine months later, though, he was back on the streets after getting fired (reportedly for not getting along well with his boss). But by now his basket of skills was much larger. Now Rutter had driving, chauffeuring, dispatching, *and* operations experience under his belt. He still had no formal business schooling, but he felt confident enough to forge ahead and make his mark. With his knowledge and know-how covering every corner of the business, he quickly envisioned a luxury transportation service that would surpass that of all of his previous employers. Finally he could call the shots and set the bar. He was ready to go out on his own. He was ready to take that dare.

In 1982 Rutter used his savings to purchase a single vehicle, launching Commonwealth Worldwide. That company now operates more than 180 vehicles (with eco-friendly hybrids now available, too). He never lost sight of his vision, providing the excellence that was missing in the industry. The values Rutter espouses in his business, and that embody his core philosophy, are summed up in four key values: accountability, communication, exceptional customer care, and professionalism. Not everyone can claim these values, but they are the keys to many successful businesses across many industries. If you can incorporate these values into your own work, you are likely to break out ahead of the competition, just like Rutter did.

A year after Rutter launched his small company in 1983, Commonwealth Worldwide earned its first of many Best of Boston awards from *Boston* magazine, which helped stimulate more business. In one month Rutter saw demand for his service triple, and the story continued as Rutter slowly built his business, one car, one chauffeur at a time.

In 2003 his company was named one of the top-ten largest limousine networks in the United States by *Limousine Digest* magazine. And in 2004 Rutter looked to the south and expanded Commonwealth Worldwide's operations into the greater New York market. To keep up with its rapidly expanding business, it moved its operations to a 20,000-square-foot garage and offices. The company is now a world leader in luxury chauffeur transportation, and in 2007 it ranked #52 on *Inc.* magazine's Inner City 100, boasting a growth rate of 248 percent between 2001 and 2005, with $21.7 million in revenues in 2005 and 270 full-time employees. It also has 400 affiliates worldwide, which account for about 40 percent of its revenue. Talk about going from taxi driver to tycoon! What's especially worthy about Rutter's business is that he chooses to run his headquarters from lower-income communities in both Boston and New York, which allows him to support the local economy and provide jobs that otherwise might not exist.

Don't underestimate the power of inner-city business. *Inc.* magazine's 2007 Inner City 100 by the Numbers analysis came up with the following figures:

- 535%: Average five-year Standard Growth Rate (median = 252%)
- 49%: Average Compound Annual Growth Rate (median = 37%)
- $39 million: Average 2005 Revenue (median = $8.3 million)
- $3.9 billion: Aggregate 2005 Revenues
- $20.7 million: Average estimated value of 2007 Inner City 100 companies
- 1994: Average year companies were founded
- 18,882: People employed by the 2007 Inner City 100 companies
- 11,839: New jobs created between 2001 and 2005

Other key features to note about these businesses is that 73 percent are in service industries; 81 percent drew from loans and credit lines for growth capital; and 68 percent seek to distinguish themselves on quality or service.

FIVE STEPS OUT OF A PROBLEM

In 2005 business writer (and successful CEO himself) Keith McFarland wrote a great article based on extensive research for *Inc.* magazine, titled "What Makes Them Tick," in which he shares some uncommon thoughts on how successful leaders think and solve problems. It's been proven, for example, that *Inc.* 500 leaders are more self-confident than 90 percent of the general population. McFarland writes that the "circumstances of the launching of their companies often means parachuting into hostile territory, often with little more than their wits and a compelling vision and the confidence to go on." What they also have in common, aside from determination, drive, and hustle, is a recipe for solving problems that they can rely upon again and

Inc. 500 CEOs scored higher than 92 percent of the population on the ability to solve problems and generate ideas, and almost 25 percent higher than other CEOs on the ability to read people and situations. Business writer Keith McFarland points out that these findings dispel a common misconception—that entrepreneurs can work miracles in the moment but lack the skills necessary to build a successful business over the long term. Much to the contrary, these CEOs have a set of skills that include quick-thinking for the short term and strategic thinking for the long term. They also have an acute awareness of their surroundings.

again. If you were to ask any great leader or business owner how he or she solves problems, I bet you'd get an earful.

So I'm going to give you my own five-step strategy for tackling problems, many of which will reinforce concepts we've already covered. It's the perfect way to end this book, instilling you with a few last tips for dealing with setbacks, failures, obstacles, and rejection—all of which inhibit our ability to invest in ourselves. When difficult circumstances arise, and trust me they will, they often happen for a reason, so pay attention to them. My five-step process works especially well for people who can't *think* their way out of a problem easily and who need a process to follow.

Don't Personalize the Problem

Problem solving means not personalizing a problem, understanding that we all go through our trials and tribulations. Life is

> **REALITY CHECK**: We're human. We have emotions. So it can be challenging to remove our personal selves and feelings from a problem. Negative thoughts can instantly crush us, making us feel like "It's all my fault, I'm bad, I'm stupid, I'll never get out of this . . ." This is when you need to not only send in some positive affirmations to the rescue, but disconnect yourself as fast as you can from the problem at hand. Otherwise the problem *will* take you down!

like a roller coaster—it has its ups and downs. If you depersonalize the problem, it becomes *a* problem instead of *your* problem. Then you can approach the problem with the perspective of "This too shall pass." Once you have placed the problem in its proper perspective, it becomes easier to resolve.

The difference is as simple as saying "My business is having difficulties—what can I do to take care of them?" as opposed to saying "My business is going under." The first statement identifies a clear problem that can be resolved, while the second statement assumes that failure is a foregone conclusion and, at that point, problem solving is useless.

It's a matter of perspective, like the old question of whether the glass is half empty or half full.

Remember, too, what I said in the previous chapter about societies that collapse: The ones who can anticipate problems and be ready to fight courageously when they occur stand a greater chance of surviving—and thriving in the long run. This holds true for businesses as well. Don't downplay problems, and whatever you do, don't ignore them. Anticipate. Respond. Stay true to your values. Adapt when circumstances tell you to. It's natural to shun dwelling on bad things that might happen. It brings us down. But those problems can veer us far off our roads and leave us in a ditch. Problems don't usually take care of themselves, so do your best to detach emotionally from them but still embrace them. Face them head-on. Besides, there's typically something to learn from them that will make you stronger and more successful.

Learn from Your Problems

Mos Def is quoted as saying, "The present is a product of the past. If you're living for now, today—without any relationship or respect for what happened yesterday—you put yourself at risk for repeating the same mistake."

When life gives you lemons—make lemonade! How many times have you heard that phrase? I'm sure you've heard it more than a few. The question is whether you have internalized it or not. Are you sitting around depressed and sucking on life's lemons, complaining about what has happened, or are you moving forward with that knowledge under your belt? We not only learn from the situations that life presents us, but from the people who are a part of those situations as well. That means that we should pay close attention to the type of people we meet, because more than likely we will meet those types of people again later in life. If we have paid attention, we will know how to deal with them. If you understand what happened yesterday, it is less likely that the same thing will go on today. I believe that if we learn enough about what we have been through and about the people we have been through it with, we can ward off future problems, solving them before they occur. If you understand clearly what happened before, you can prevent it from re-occurring.

To me life is a classroom. It doesn't matter if the situation involves family, friends, relationships, or business—there is always something to learn. Once I have examined a situation and have processed it all internally, I have graduated from that class and have a degree in that situation. When I encounter that situation again, I will be able to work from the inside out.

For example, if you eat strawberries and have a severe allergic reaction to them, you would be smart to avoid strawberries. Business situations are no different. If you are in business with someone who has cheated you out of money, the best thing to do would be to end the business relationship. And sometimes you can learn from what is happening right now. For example, if you know that the market for entertainment attorneys is saturated, you would be smart to switch your emphasis to business law or perhaps pursue another career.

Being a Cold-Blooded Realist

If you don't recall my notes on this one, go back to Chapter 5, where you got a healthy dose of how being a cold-blooded realist can be a saving grace. Look for fantasies behind the fairy tales. Reject the lies of the rich and famous. Be real about what's really there and what's not. Don't take paths to mirages. Find facts amid fictions. Do as many reality checks as you need to. And again, anticipate potential problems like a chess player and fight them like a sumo wrestler.

Being a cold-blooded realist will force you to deal with problems. It will also help you to acknowledge when there is a problem and to proceed to seek solutions. When a problem arises, you may want to fool yourself and pretend it's not there, but when you're not being real about it, it will be difficult—if not impossible—to resolve anything.

Many people will avoid reality by lying to themselves, saying, "I don't have a problem." But that doesn't make the problem go away. You can't just close your eyes and think that the world no longer exists, because as soon as you open your eyes again, the cold-blooded reality will be waiting to pass you a beatdown!

I live my life running *to* reality as opposed to running *from* reality. I call this being a cold-blooded realist. Whatever the reality is, I go after it and handle it accordingly. Consider this: You can spend a great deal of time (and energy, inspiration, motivation) looking for ways to avoid a problem or to get around it, but it's far more practical simply to face it and begin to find solutions. Only then will you learn from the problem and move forward a stronger, richer person.

Attack the Plan

Once you have analyzed the problem and placed it in its proper perspective, you can formulate a plan of attack and, well, attack it! Think of yourself as the general of a great army of soldiers, dedicated to attacking the enemy at all costs. Remember, this is your life at stake, and your success—your own little society—depends on your actions.

INVEST IN YOURSELF FIRST

I've been talking about the idea of investing in yourself throughout this book. But since we're covering the subject of investing, I want to reiterate this point, even at the expense of repetition. It's not always easy to invest in ourselves. There's a lot at risk when we put ourselves out there emotionally, spiritually, and physically. But these human elements are part of the success equation.

While we like to *think* we are investing in ourselves every day, the truth of the matter is we don't. All too often we let the poison of everyday life—the stress, the bills, the bosses, other people's vision, and the craziness of a 24–7 society—take over and rot our motivation and inspiration to move closer to our goals and dreams. We don't take time to read books and learn new things: We don't permit ourselves to have a time out so we can give back to ourselves through rest and relaxation. We don't stop to feed ourselves the kind, cheerful words we want to hear from that voice inside. Instead we let life lull us into a robotic, semicomplacent state in which we don't have access to our dreams and goals. This is when you begin hearing "I can't, I can't, I can't" play over and over again with no end in sight. I can't go to the gym. I can't start my own business. I can't think about another career. I can't get out of debt. I can't go back to school. I can't find my purpose. I can't be rich. I can't . . . I can't . . . I can't . . .

Here's what I have to say about that: YES YOU CAN.

REALITY CHECK: If you don't go within, you go without. You deserve to get to where you want to be, period.

Consider this: If your personal bank account is worth billions, imagine what you would be able to materialize in your outer world. But if your personal inventory is low—and you are not doing the things you love, guess what? You probably won't be rich by any stretch of that word. Like the old saying goes, life is not a dress rehearsal. This is the one life you're given, so you'd best show up for yourself first. I often ask people whether they are happy and operating at 100 percent. When they get defensive and brusquely respond, "Yeah, I'm happy," I don't believe them. And if they are not lying to themselves they are lying to somebody. We all possess parts of ourselves that we would like to enhance—if not, we wouldn't be human.

So here's my message: Each day dedicate a percentage of yourself to your goals and dreams. It will add up over time. Remember, discipline weighs ounces but regrets weigh tons. If you don't have discipline, you have nothing—you need discipline to be an effective individual. People tend to forget the importance of focused discipline when they're in the rut of daily life. Devoting a percentage of time to your vision can be as simple as going to a physical place that recharges your batteries and allows you to reflect. It's where you concentrate on honing in on and paying attention to your talents and skills. It can be a favorite chair in your home, a bedroom, a spot on the beach, or at a corner café. This is the place where you can let your thoughts and feelings roam free. You are not a prisoner of life here. Much to the contrary, you feel an incredible sense of empowerment and the time seems appropriate to ask yourself those three questions:

> *Who am I?*
> *What am I becoming?*
> *Am I happy with who I am?*

If you do this self-examination often, it will have the effect of building YOU up and it will give you more clarity. It will also help you to take inventory of your life and make tiny shifts in the way you talk to yourself. When we fail to check in with ourselves routinely, we begin to fall into cycles of negative thinking and a self-defeating mentality. With every pessimistic thought that enters our minds comes a bruise to our sense of self-worth and self-esteem, which begins to chip away at our subconscious, which then translates to the conscious decisions we make. And we all know what that ultimately means. It means we either get to where we want to be or not. Succeed or fail. Live richly or live poorly.

> My interest is in the future, because I am going to spend the rest of my life there.
>
> —CHARLES KETTERING

EPILOGUE

Be You and Be Real

*Some men see things as they are and say, "Why?" I dream things that never were and say, "Why **not**?"*

I didn't write this book for you so you could achieve my level of success. I wrote it as a catalyst to get you to identify why God put you on this Earth. And I hope your success will be ten times greater than mine. I don't want you to be rich, I want you to be *richer*. Don't make me or anyone else your aspiration. Dream beyond. Be your own aspiration through finding your area of excellence and having the confidence to go with it. I wholeheartedly believe that if you are passionate about your work, you'll discover things that aren't intuitive to others but are fairly obvious to you. Which is exactly why you needn't let fear, worry, doubt, and anxiety consume you. Confidence, courage, and a consistent amount of effort and dedication will get you to where you want to be.

If I were to sum up my central life philosophy, it would be this: When you are living real, with your heart in the right place, and you're investing in ideas and people—including yourself— then you are going to be a success in life.

What other lies are holding you back? What do you say to yourself that feeds feelings of self-doubt and worthlessness? Or that prevent you from getting to where you want to be? See if you can come up with a few more statements you find yourself hearing and that likely defeat you subconsciously. Also finish the sentence with ". . . to be rich." Note how that makes you feel! Some examples:

I'm too tired . . . to be rich.
I'm too unfit and out of shape . . . to be rich.
I'm too stressed out . . . to be rich.
I'm too uneducated . . . to be rich.
I'm too overwhelmed with family and work . . . to be rich.
I'm too depressed . . . to be rich.

Now go back and insert the word NOT after "I'm" in each of your phrases. Write them down—use a red pen if you want.

At the end of your day, when you stand in judgment of yourself or are judged by the all-knowing, what will you report as your contribution to mankind? Never forget that success is not measured by the magnitude of that contribution. Maybe you won't find the cure for AIDS or design the human-carrying rocketship to Mars. You might not become a president of any-thing or be a movie star. And maybe you won't make a great deal of money. There is more than one way to define personal success.

Today it's impossible to be a well-informed citizen without at least some knowledge of how governmental economic policies affect our ability to earn a living and provide for our future. The Federal Reserve chairman is arguably the most powerful figure in the global economy, but the effects of the popularized trickle-down economics theory may never reach or benefit you and your neighborhood. Yet the chairman's decisions directly affect our financial lives in a way no other public figure can match. He is a policymaker more powerful than the president of the United States, but information about the man himself, his beliefs, and his actions inside the Federal Reserve can be hard to come by.

Don't turn full responsibility for your personal economic affairs over to a stranger. The Federal Reserve chairman is someone you only know from news media and sound bites that you see when flipping through television channels. The buck must stop with YOU.

We live in the world's fastest-paced society. Many call it a "microwave" society, which consumes our thoughts and redirects our focus. We are hardwired to access every impulse and instantly satisfy every whimsical desire. We also may feel programmed to feel subordinate or inferior in society. Some of us are descendants of people who were transported unwillingly to this country and forcibly assigned to lives of complete servitude. We were the "children of a lesser God" who (like so much livestock) served as "beasts of burden" to those who did not value our lives. The residual ramifications can still affect us in more ways than one today, even though we do enjoy a life of abundance and access to so many things others don't have.

Black people in the United States still live and work in better conditions than millions around the world. This is not Darfur, nor is it the "Sunny Side of the Street," from an old song my grandmother used to play for me. To quote Dr. Martin Luther King: "He who starts behind in the great race of life must forever remain behind or run faster than the man in front. The demands of history require that we be as productive, as resourceful, and as responsible as the people who never had these [our historical] disadvantages."

Sometimes we move too fast for our own good or for the good of those around us. Caught up in a footrace through life, we race past the signals that are there to tell us what we need to do for ourselves or what our spouses, children, or friends need from us. Psychologists know that manic (mentally erratic) behavior is often an avoidance tactic—a way of escaping from problems and the pain that accompanies them. To someone with manic tendencies, the stimulus of frenzied activity provides a protective shield from pain. We all know people who are like this to varying degrees, because we live in a manic society. To be more in touch with real life, we need to slow down. Some of us are beginning to do just that. Only then can we begin to see our full potential, identify our purpose, nourish our innate talents and skills, and visualize a path toward success.

When it comes to charting your course for financial success, by now you know I strongly believe in self-reliance. Don't let the buck stop somewhere else. View your personal goals and ideas—

whatever they might be—as belonging solely to you. Don't let anyone steal your sense of worth or beat down the perceived value of your dreams. Excuse the cliché, but you just can't give up even when others tell you to. The great Thomas Edison was branded as a crazy man by his friends and family, yet he forged onward and invented more than a thousand devices, including the phonograph and long-lasting lightbulb. In fact, he is considered one of the most prolific inventors in history, holding 1,093 patents in the United States as well as many others in the United Kingdom, France, and Germany. (Trivia: Edison is even credited for creating the word *hello* as a telephone greeting in 1877. *Hello* is a variant of the old word "*hollo*.") For Edison, the word *failure* didn't exist. I'd venture to guess that for every invention he had, there were hundreds if not thousands of disappointments and no-go's. Persistence and tenacity were his hallmarks. So was his ability to problem solve.

You know I love a good quote. Abraham Lincoln's famous statement sums up much of how I think: "Things may come to those who wait, but only the things left by those who hustle." Hustle is focusing your dreams into fruition. Hustle is staying with it after everyone else has given up. Hustle, in the success world, is simply believing in yourself, creating a plan, and hustling along until you score points and move closer to your goal.

Think again about the lies I've discussed throughout this book. Which one is holding you back the most? Reread that chapter and then make at least one change today toward removing that lie from your vocabulary. Move out of your comfort zone. And when someone asks why, be quick to respond, with a smile, *why not?*

ABOUT FARRAH GRAY

Farrah Gray was named one of the most influential black men in America by the National Urban League's *Urban Influence* magazine. At twenty-one years old, he was recognized by *Ebony* magazine as an entrepreneurial icon, business mogul, and bestselling author. Raised in the impoverished South Side of Chicago, Farrah defied the odds and became a self-made millionaire by the age of fourteen. At the age of twenty-one, he became Dr. Farrah Gray, receiving an Honorary Doctorate of Humane Letters from Allen University in recognition of his ingenious economic mind and distinguished commitment to the development of values such as leadership, integrity, and scholarship. In his rise from poverty to national and international prominence as an entrepreneurial icon and preeminent power speaker, Farrah has inspired millions around the world.

Today Farrah addresses more than half a million people a year on topics including leadership, personal development, diversity, strategic planning, creativity, business development, and financial management. At the age of twenty-three, he has achieved more than many achieve in a lifetime. Publisher and editor-in-chief of *Prominent* magazine (www.ProminentMagazine.com), he is also a syndicated columnist with the National Newspaper Publishers Association (NNPA) federation with its two hundred weekly newspapers and more than 15 million readers. He is a dedicated AOL Money Coach, sharing advice with millions of AOL subscribers daily, and he is recognized in the Marquis *Who's Who in America.*